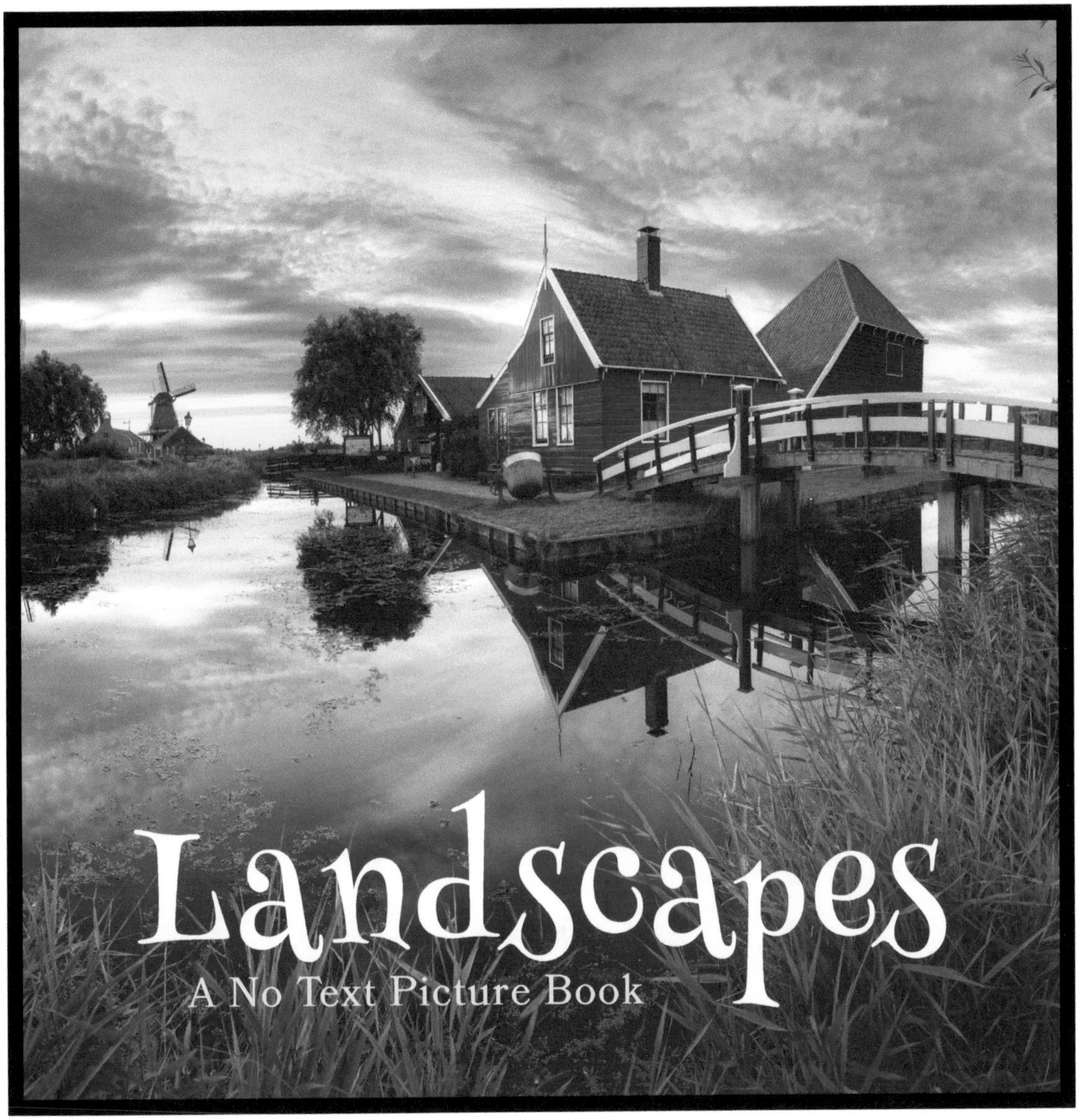

ISBN: 978-1-990181-32-0

To:

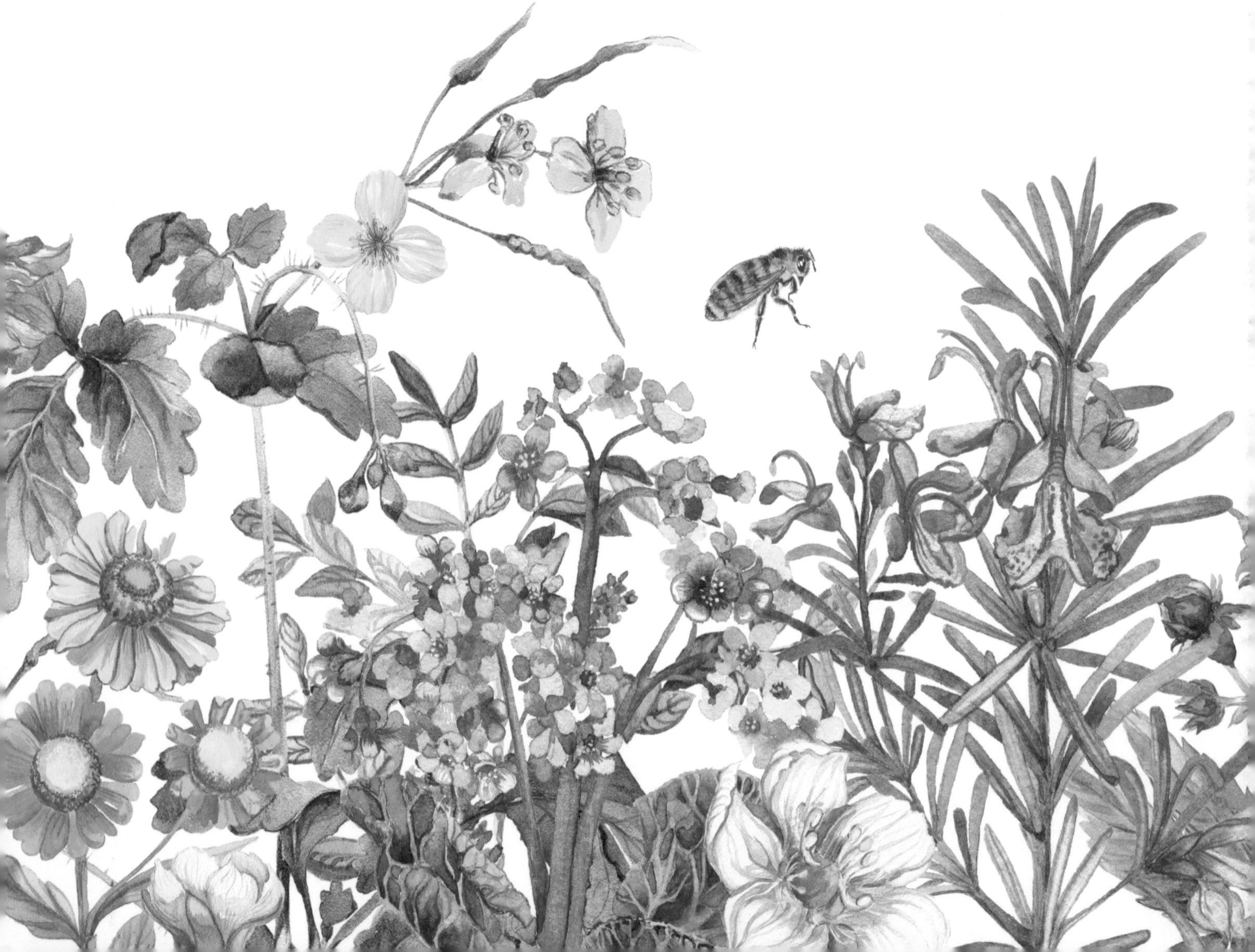

From:

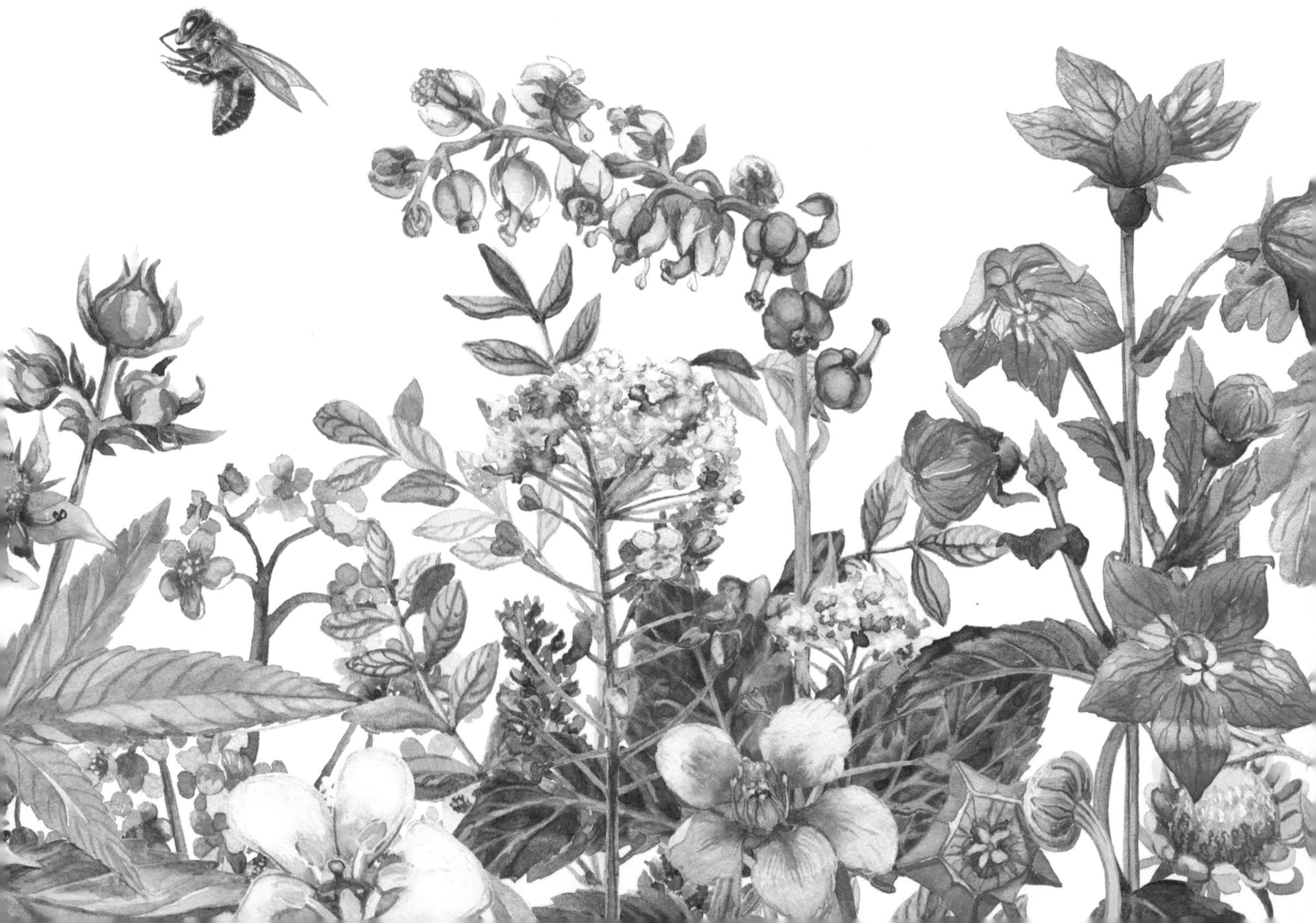

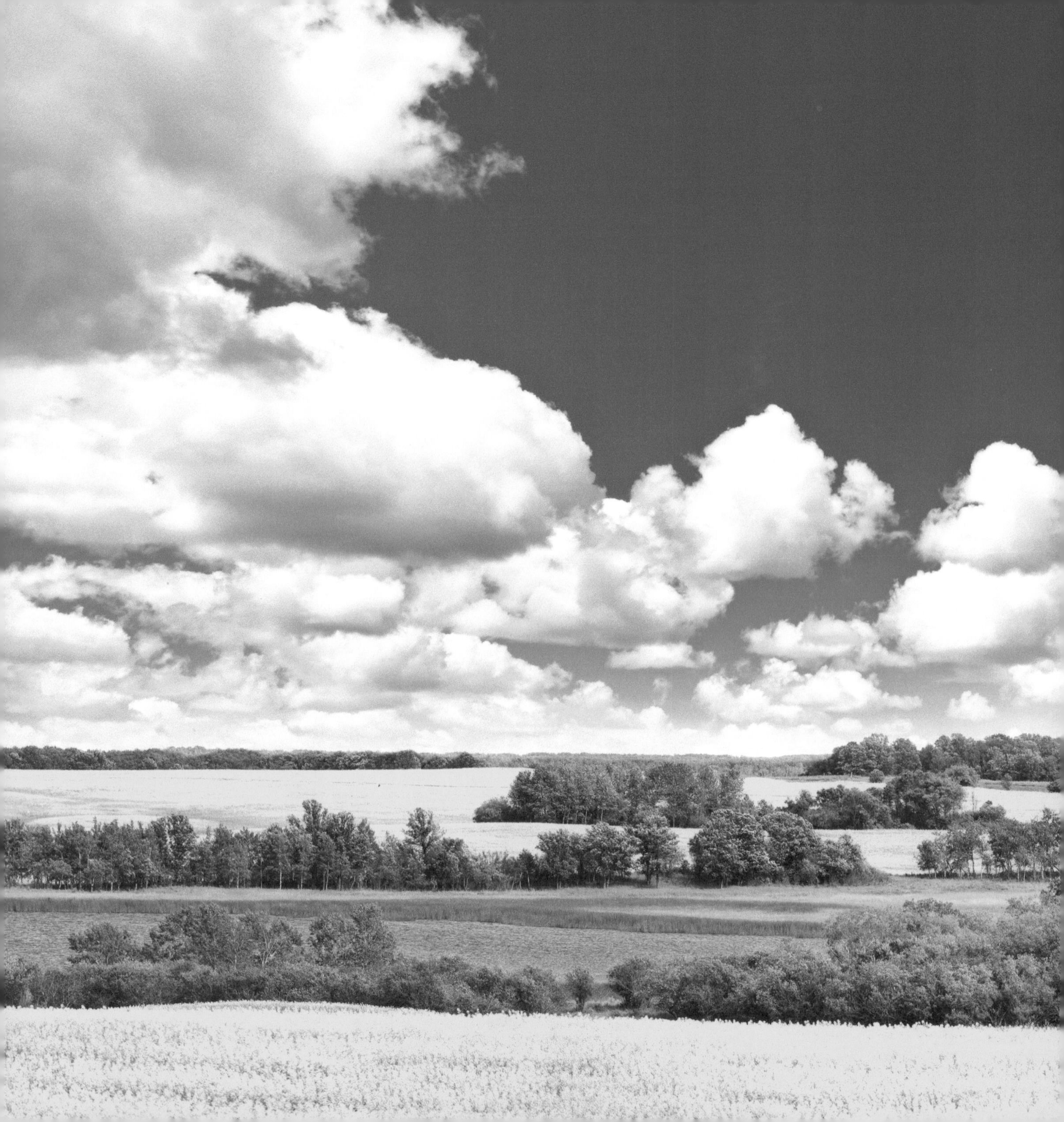

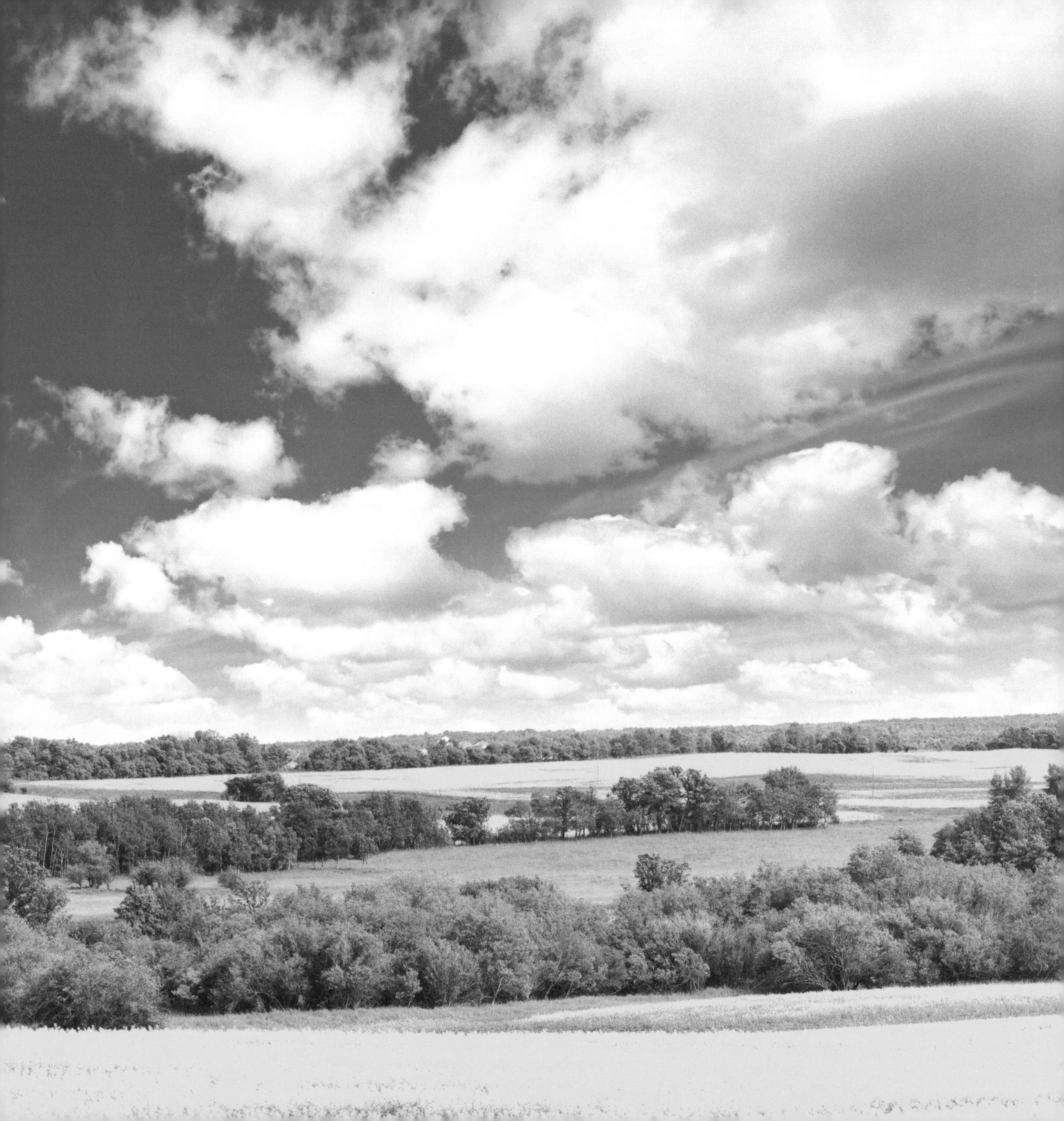

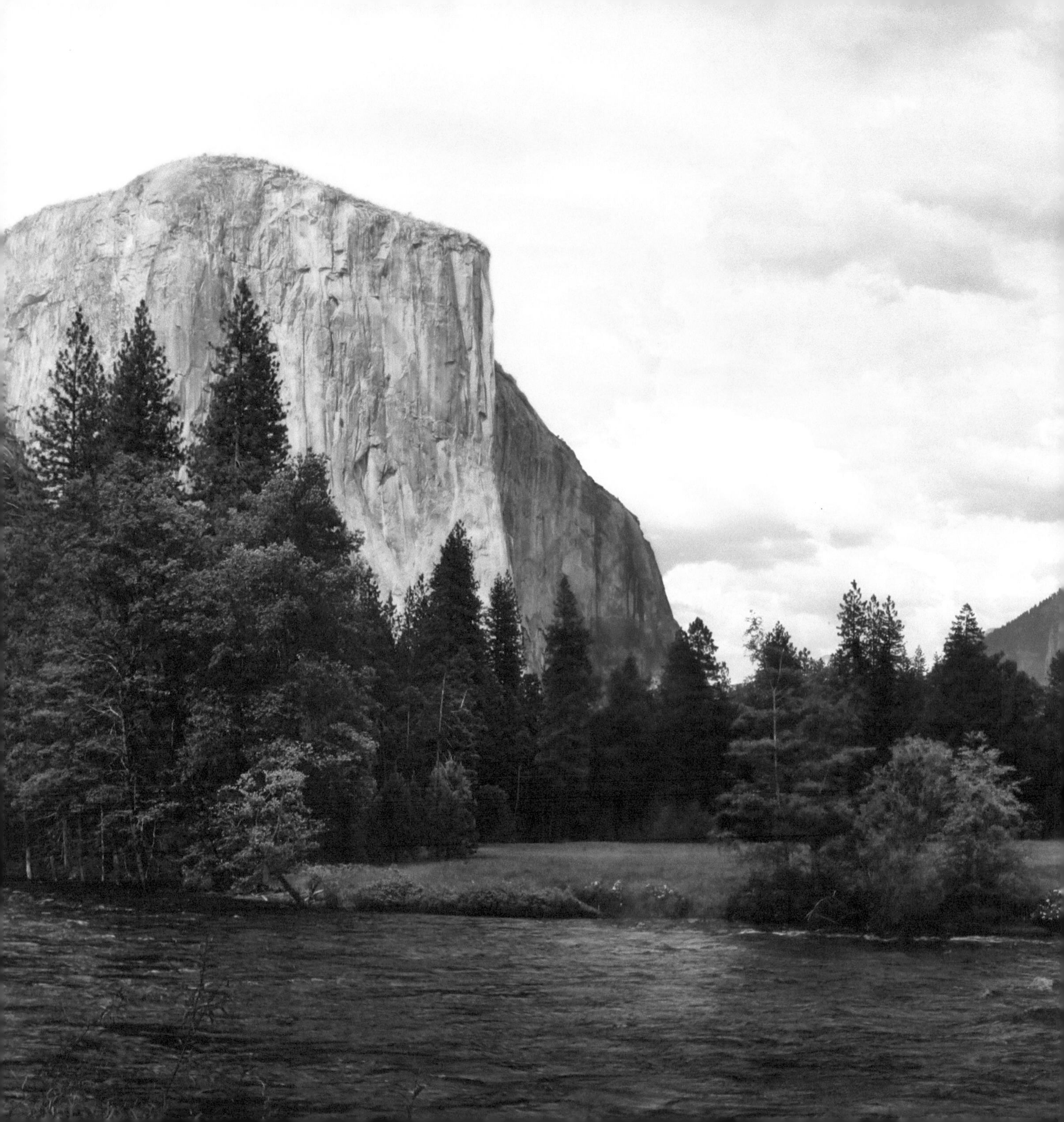

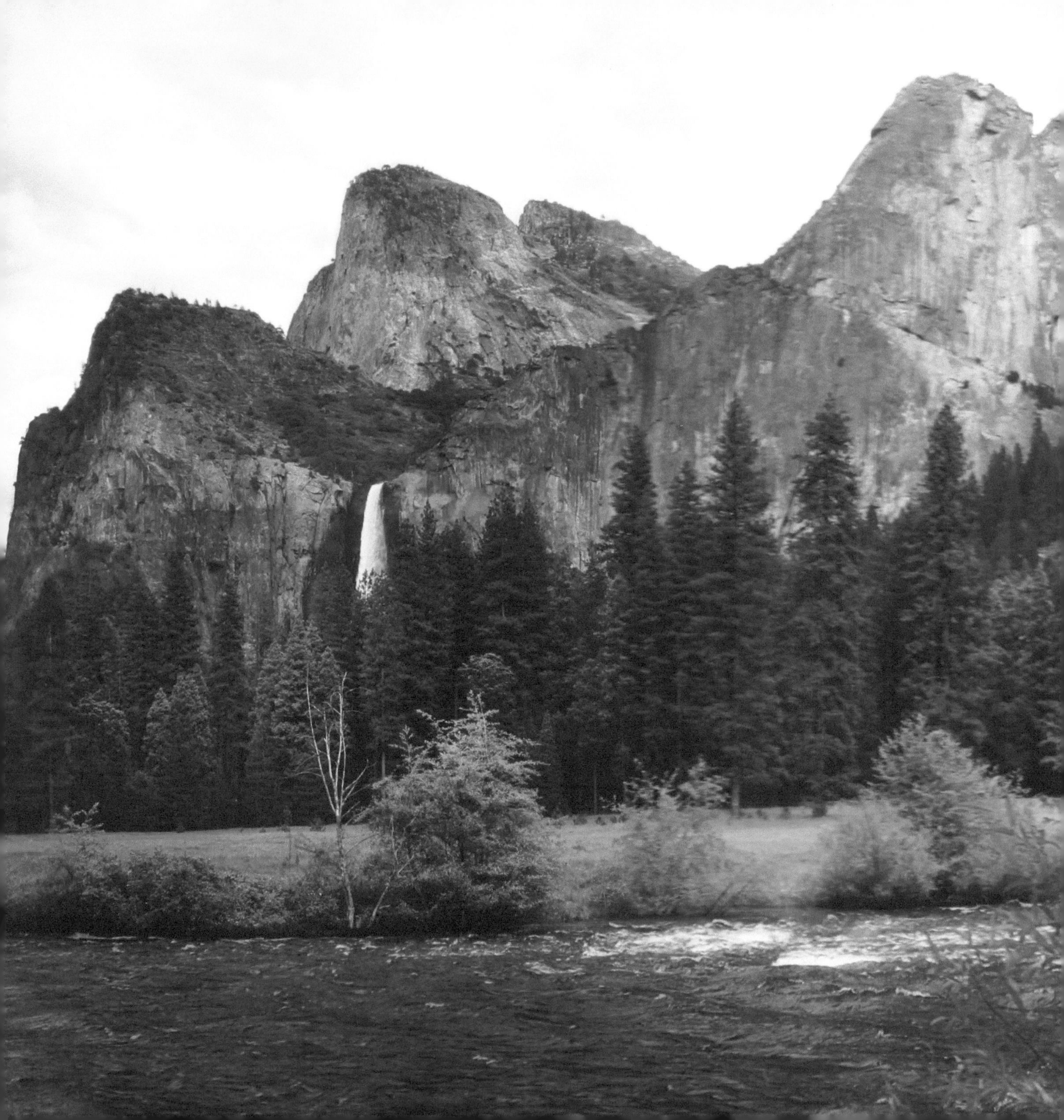

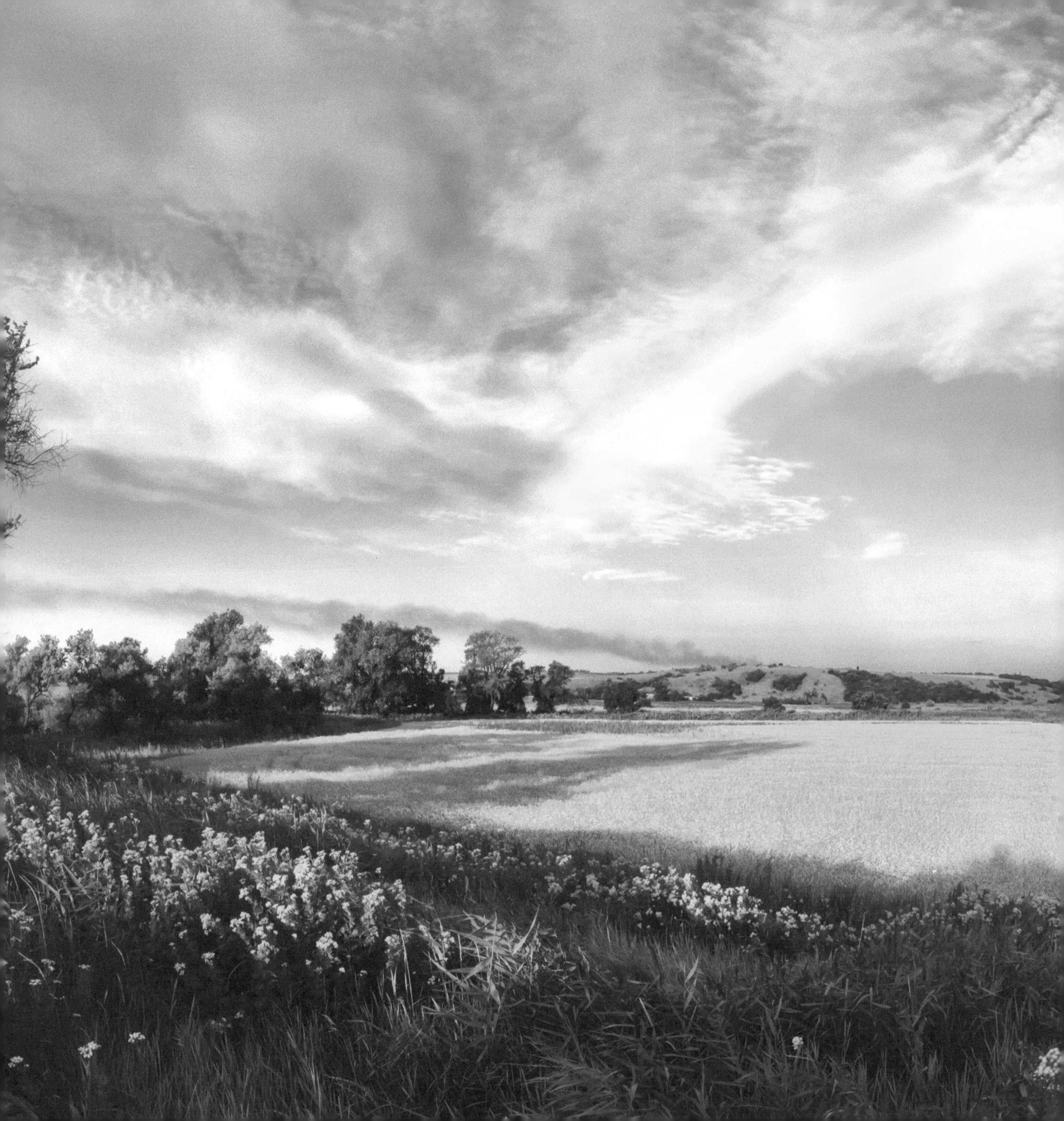

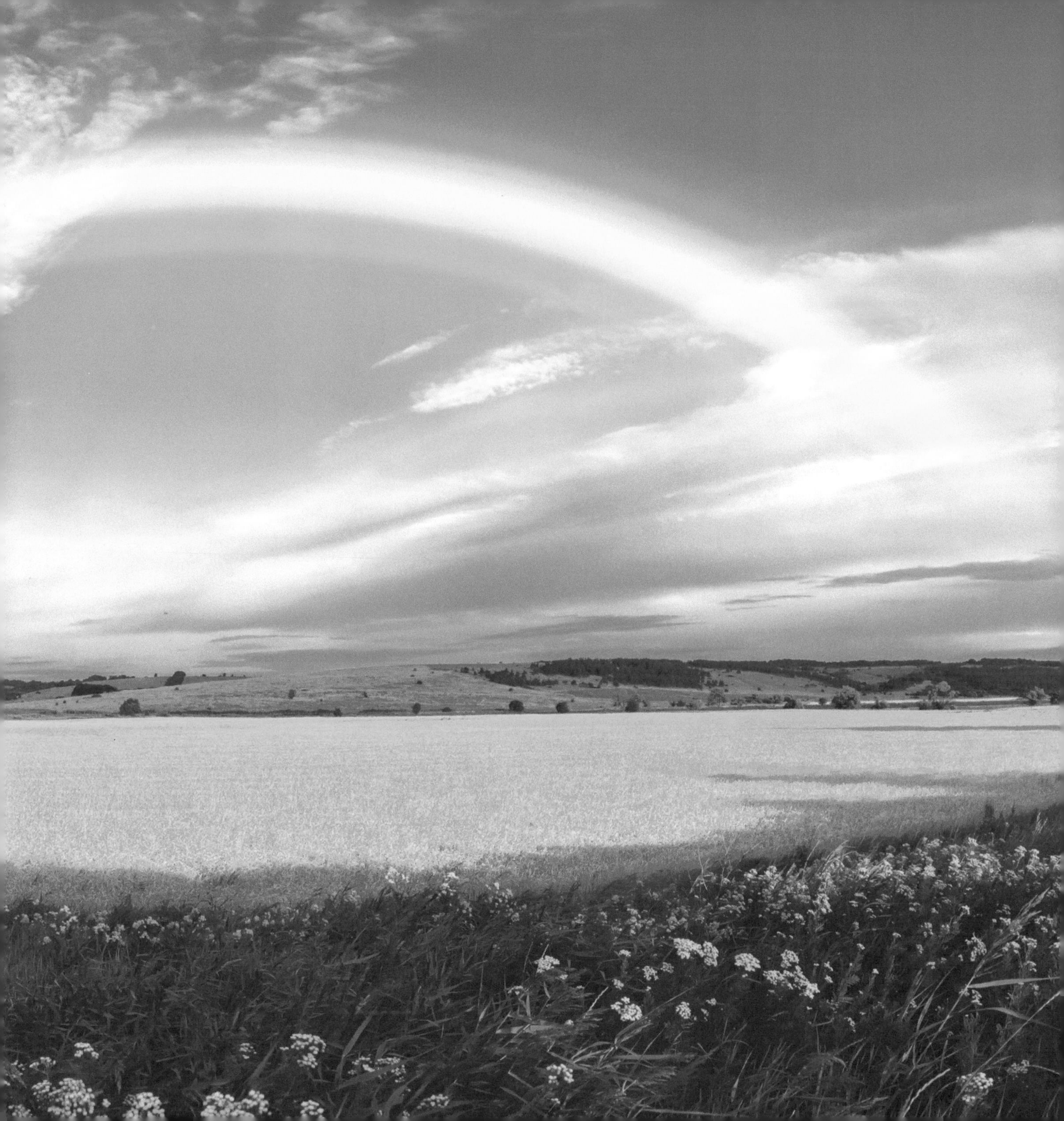

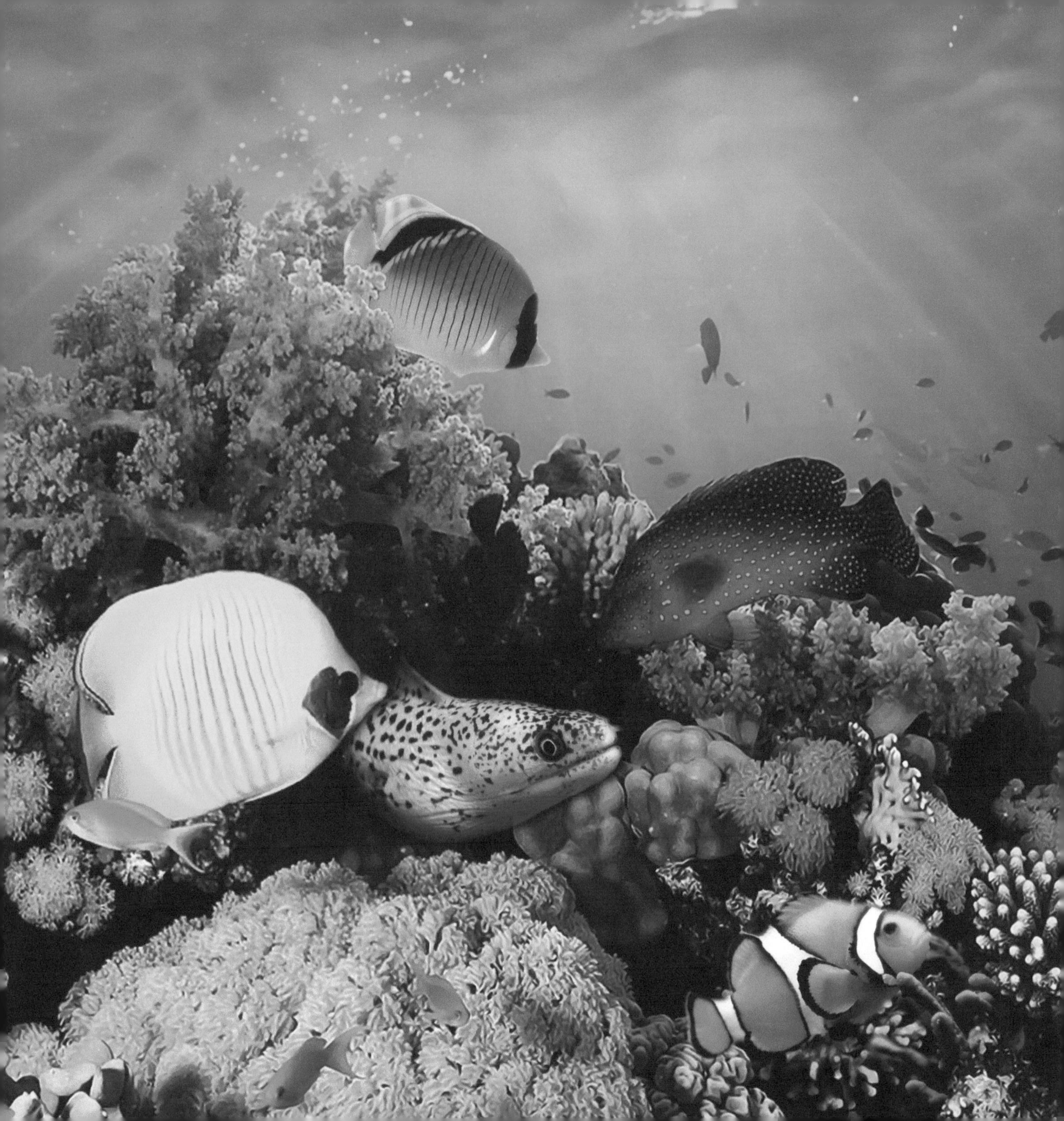

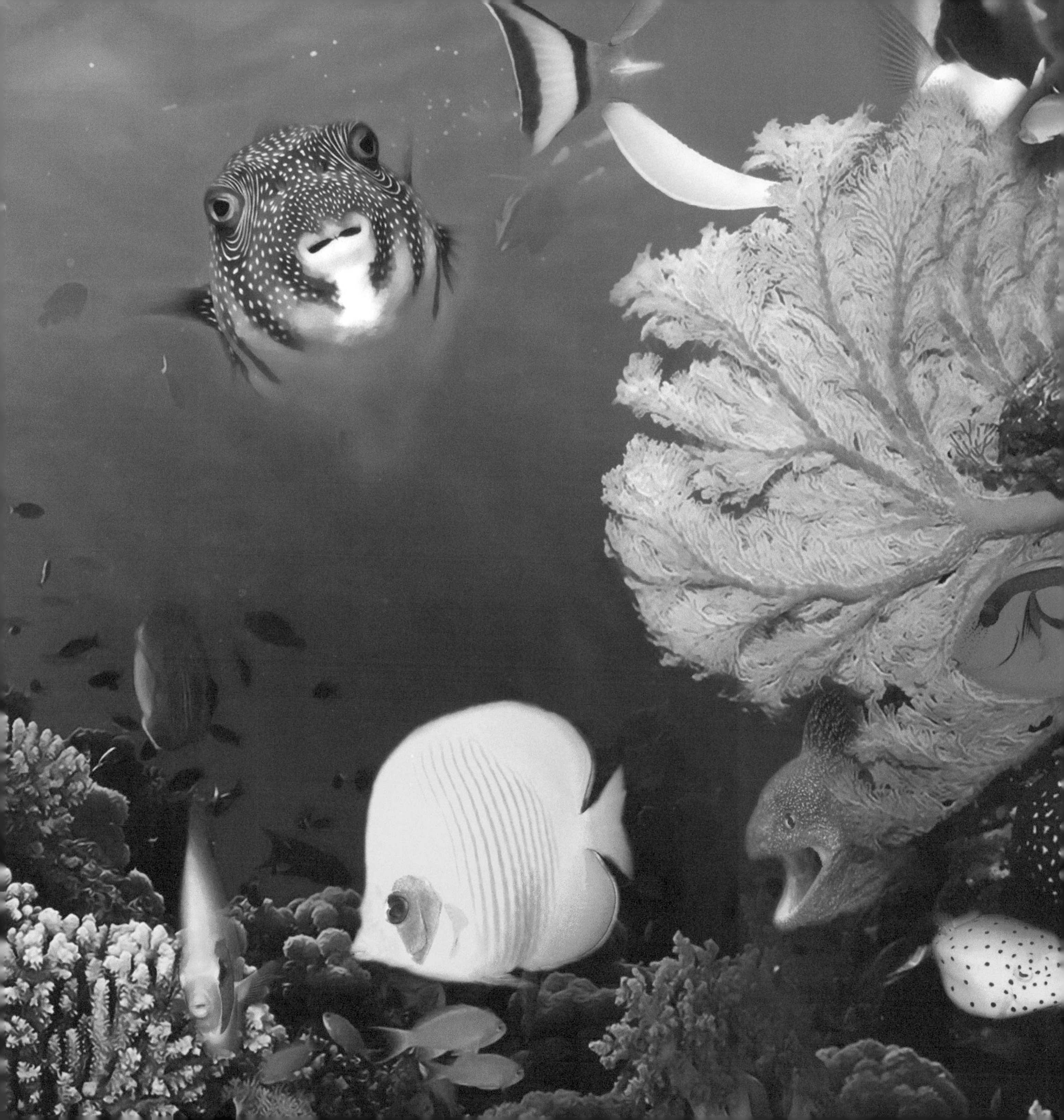

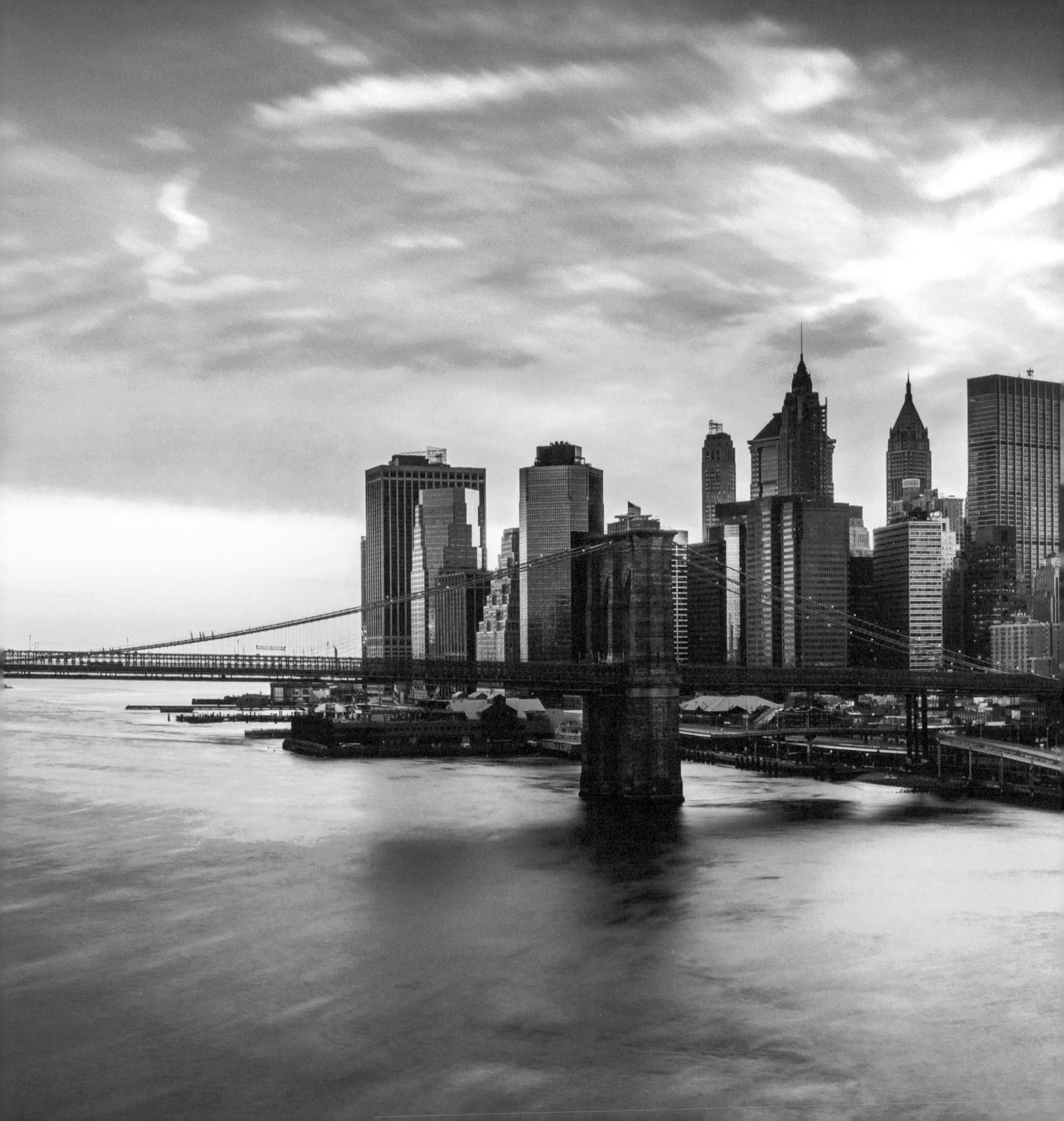

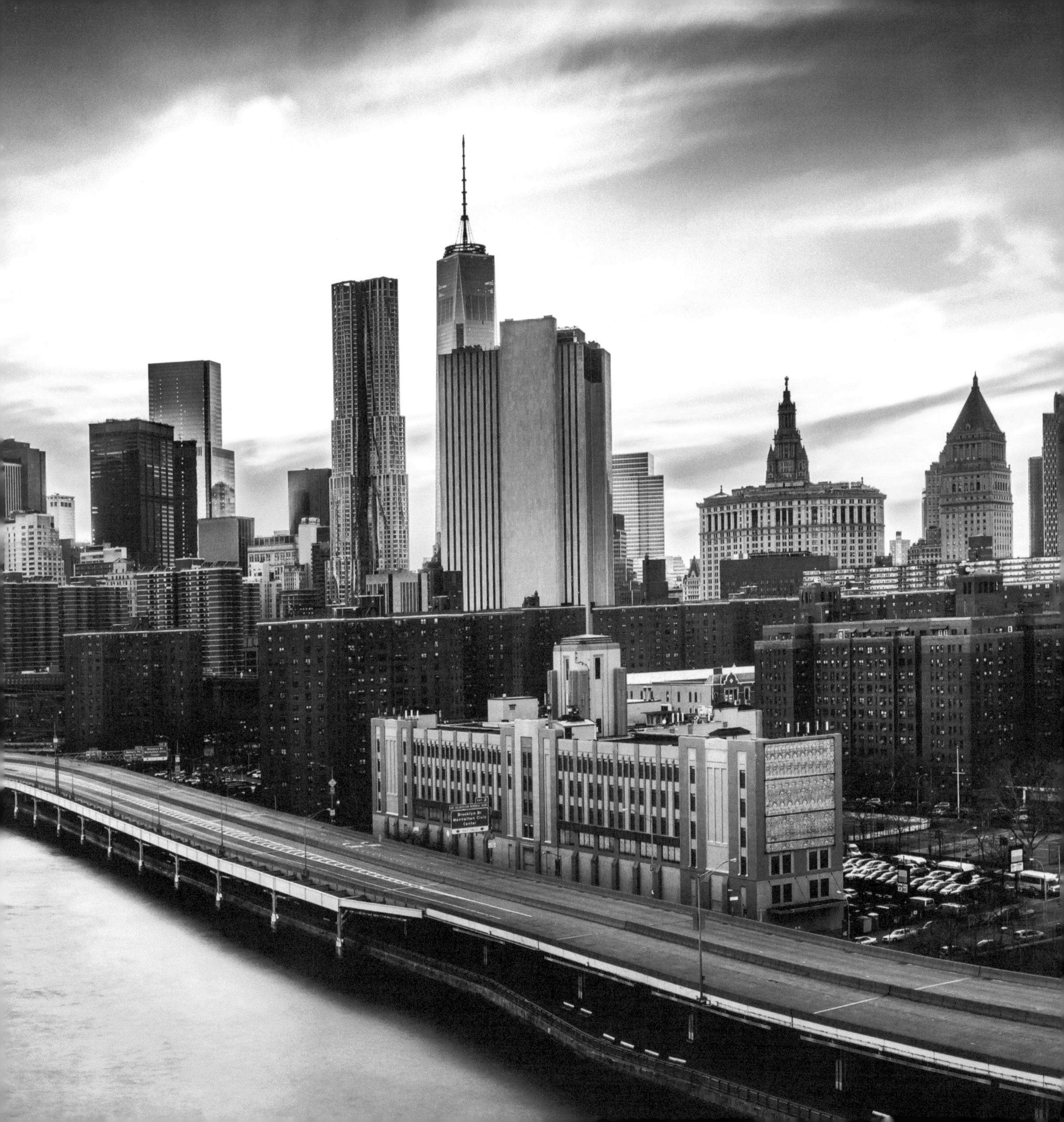
Brooklyn Br
Manhattan Civic
Center

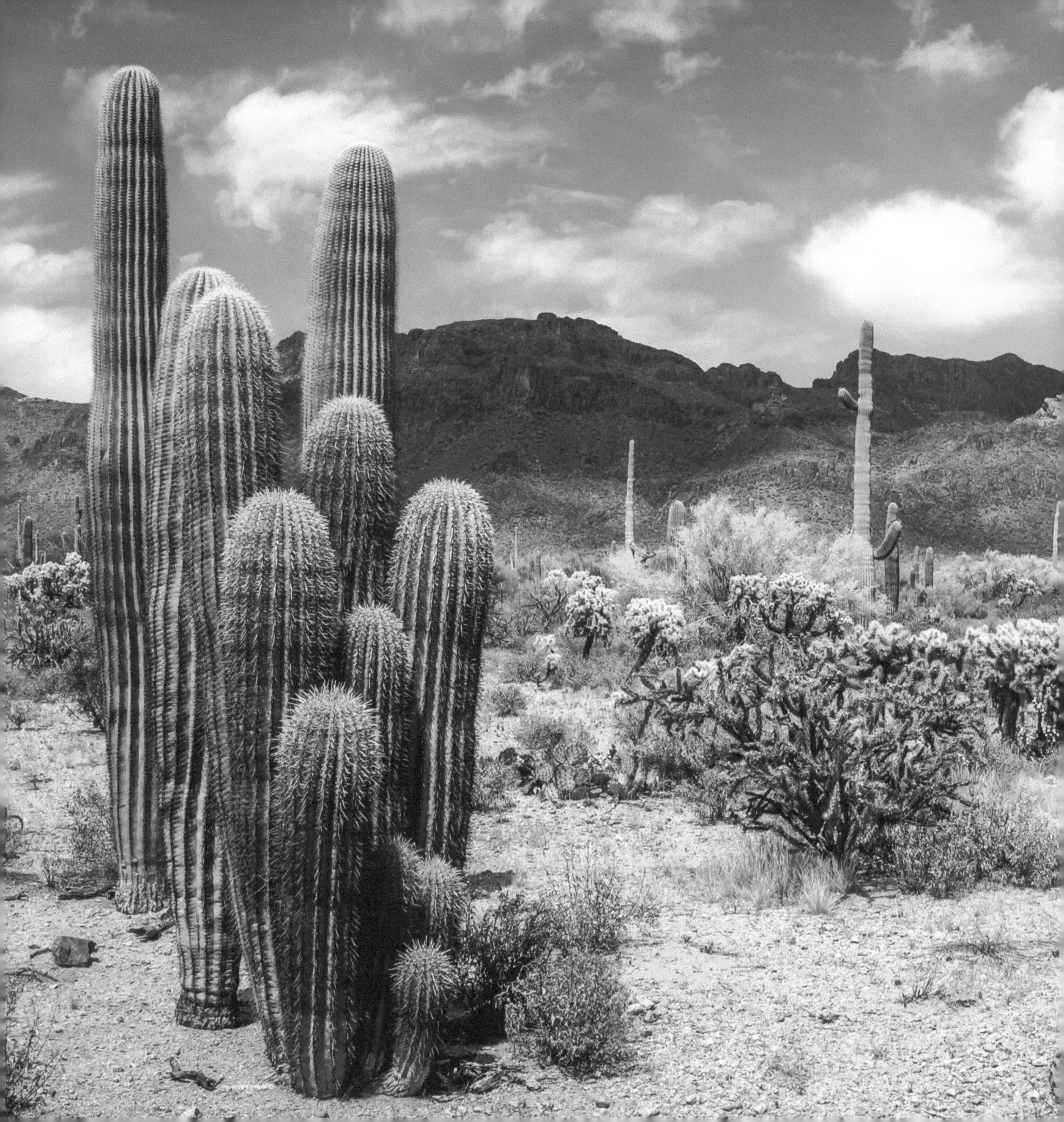

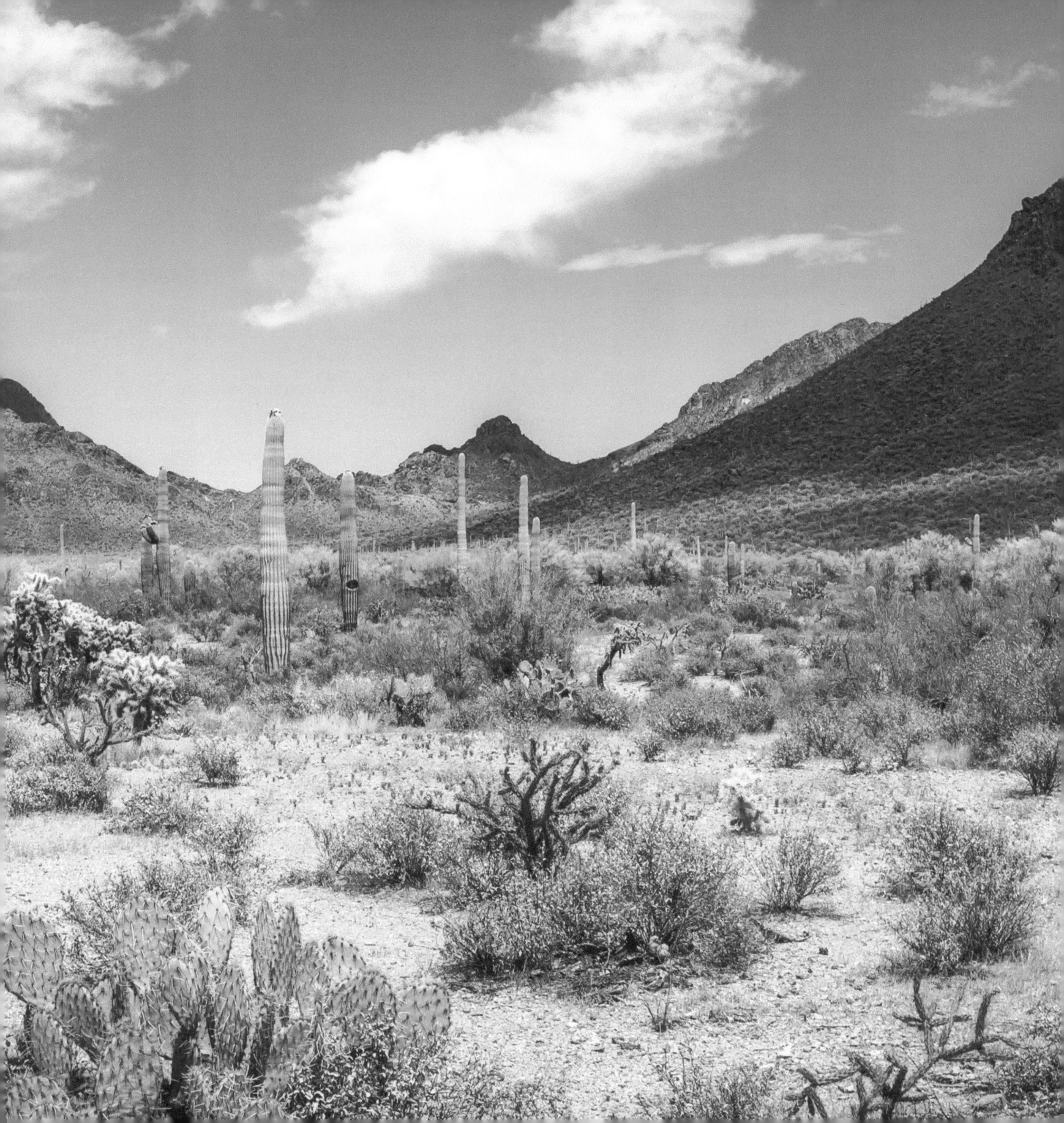

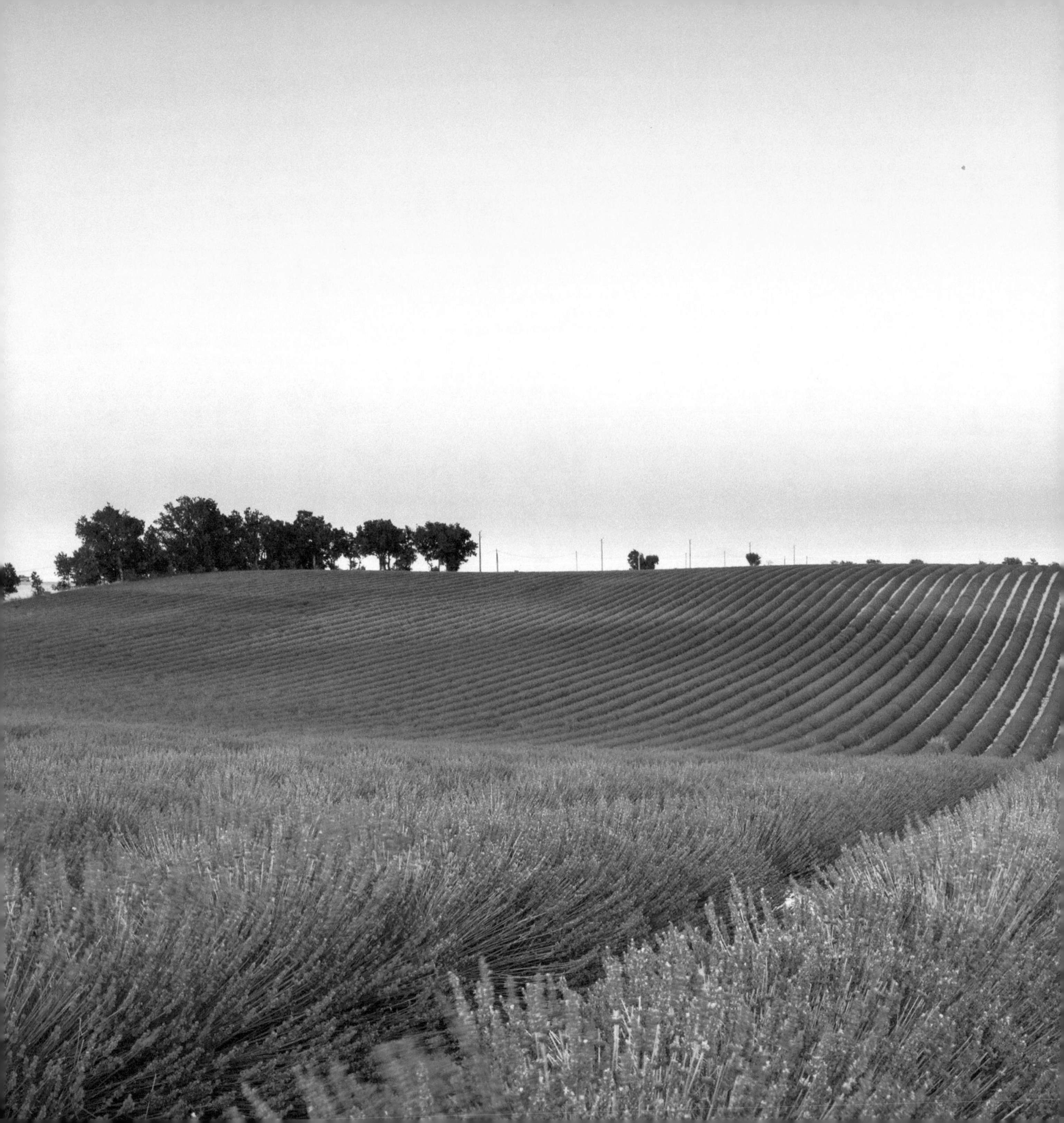

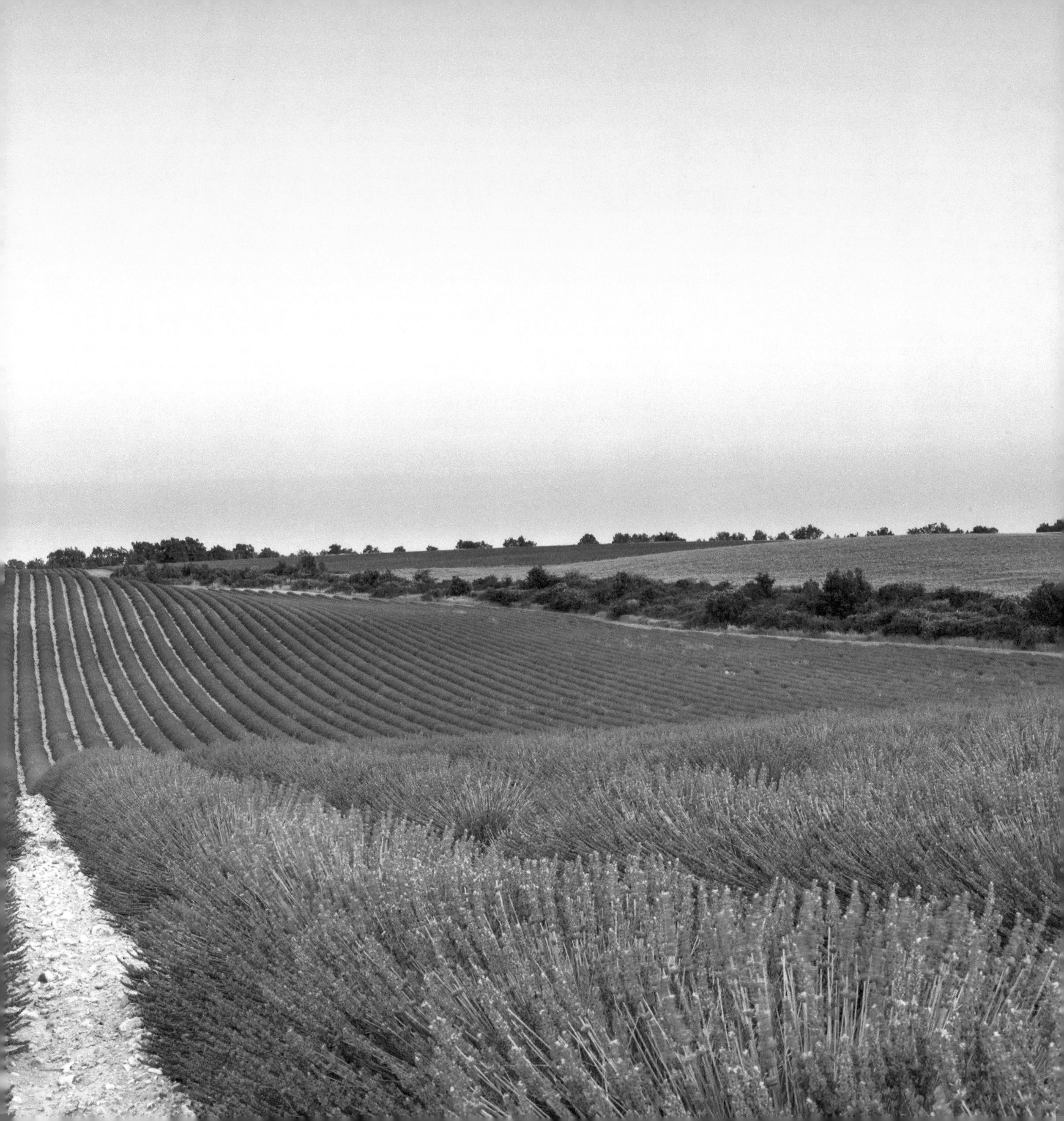

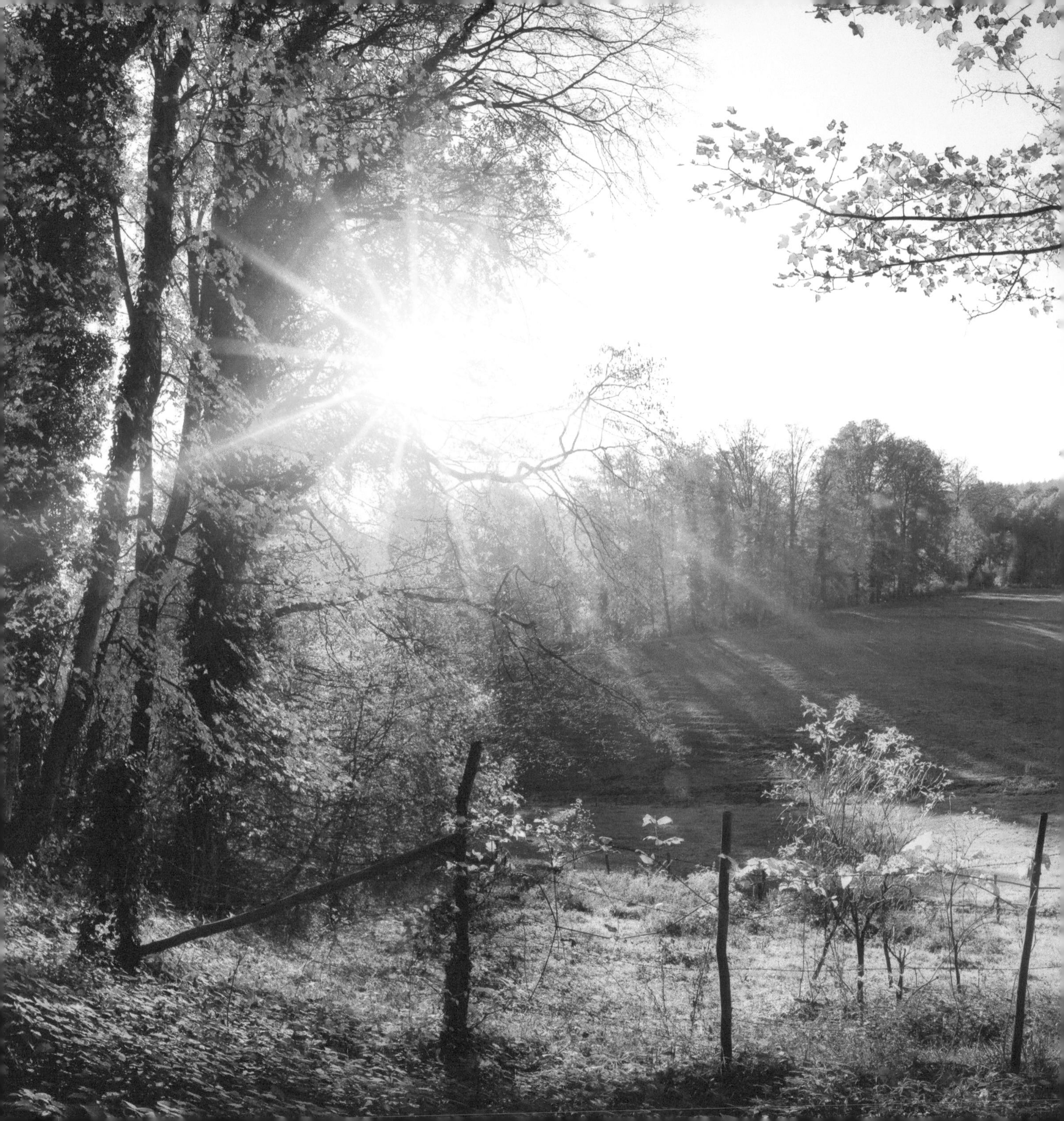

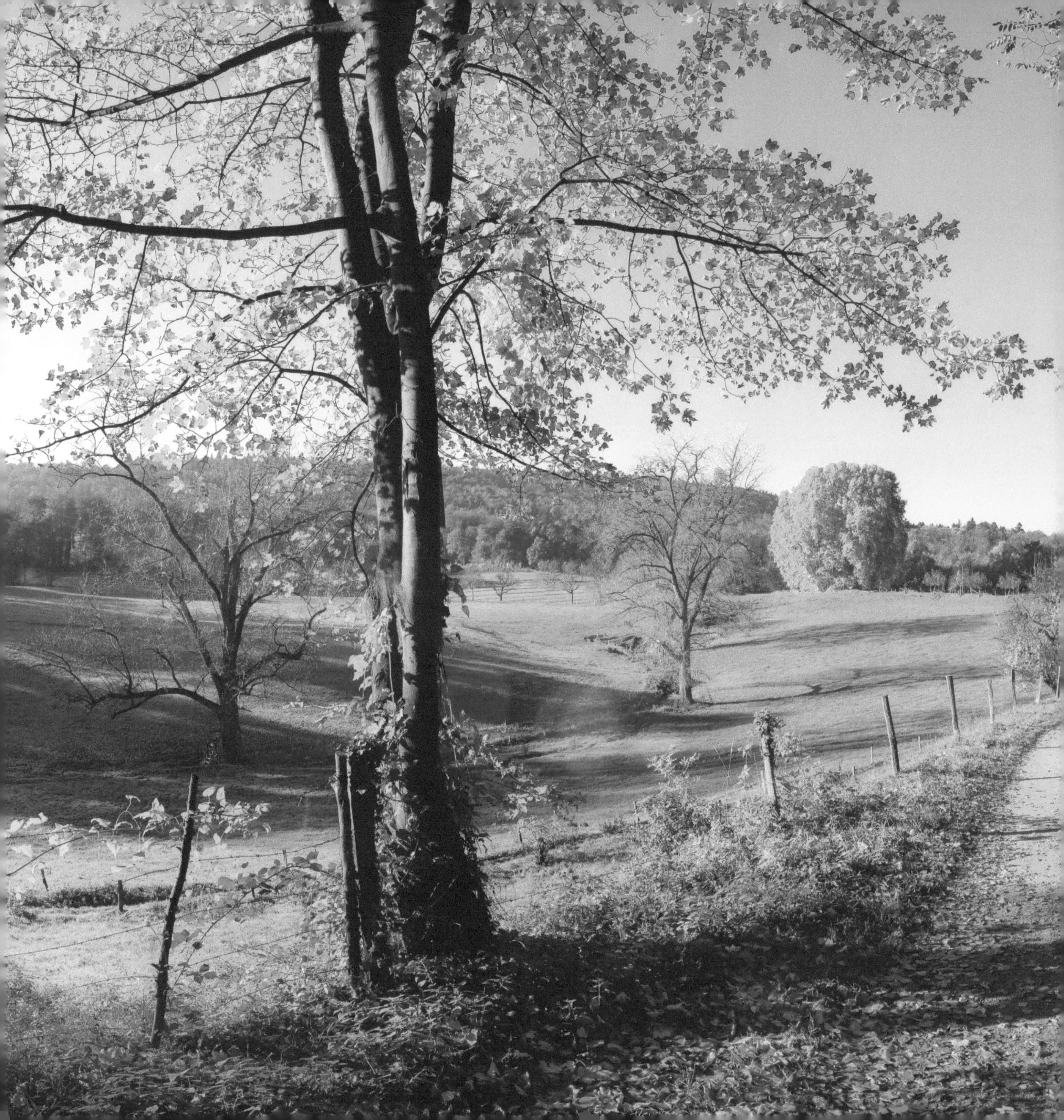

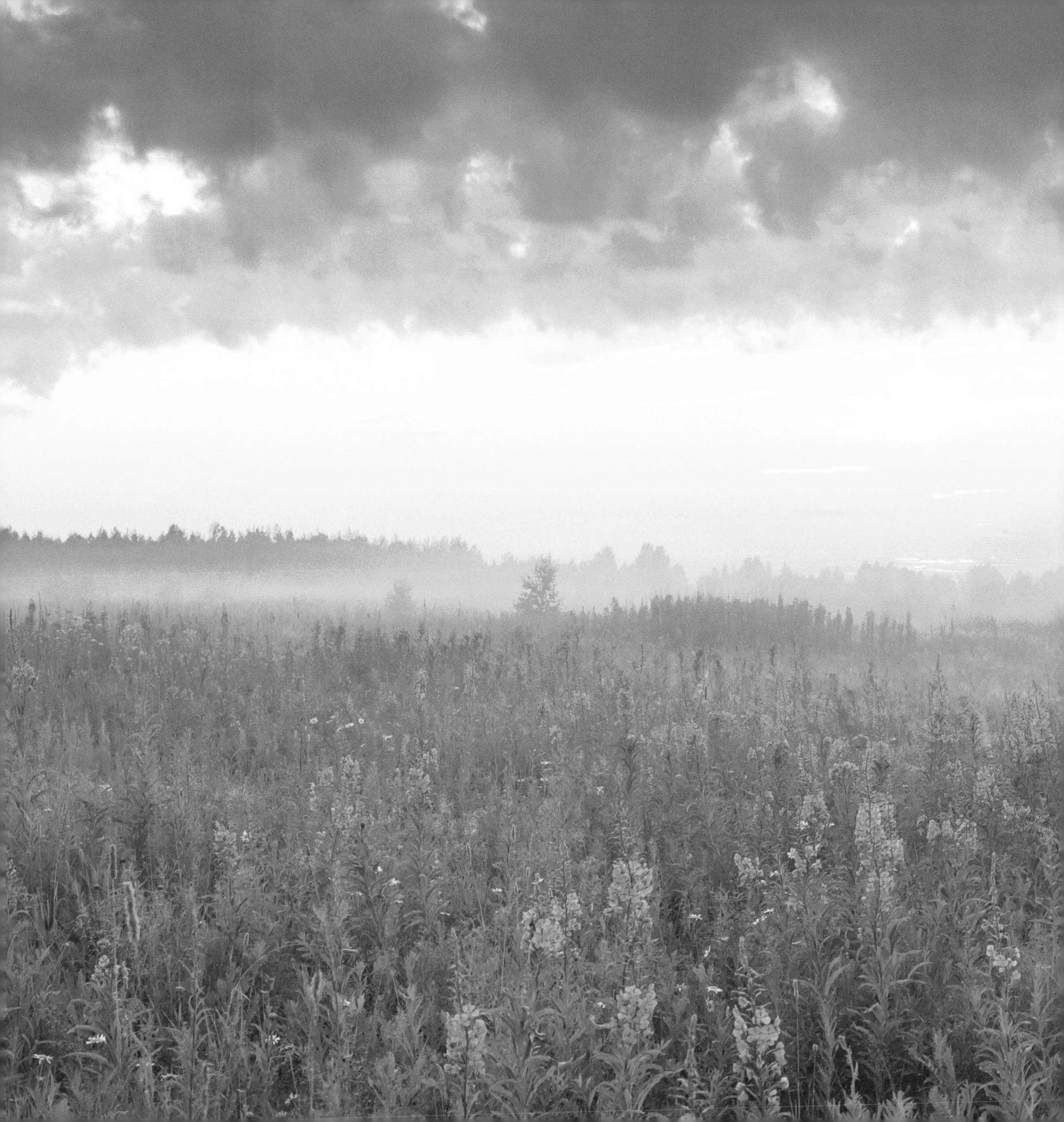

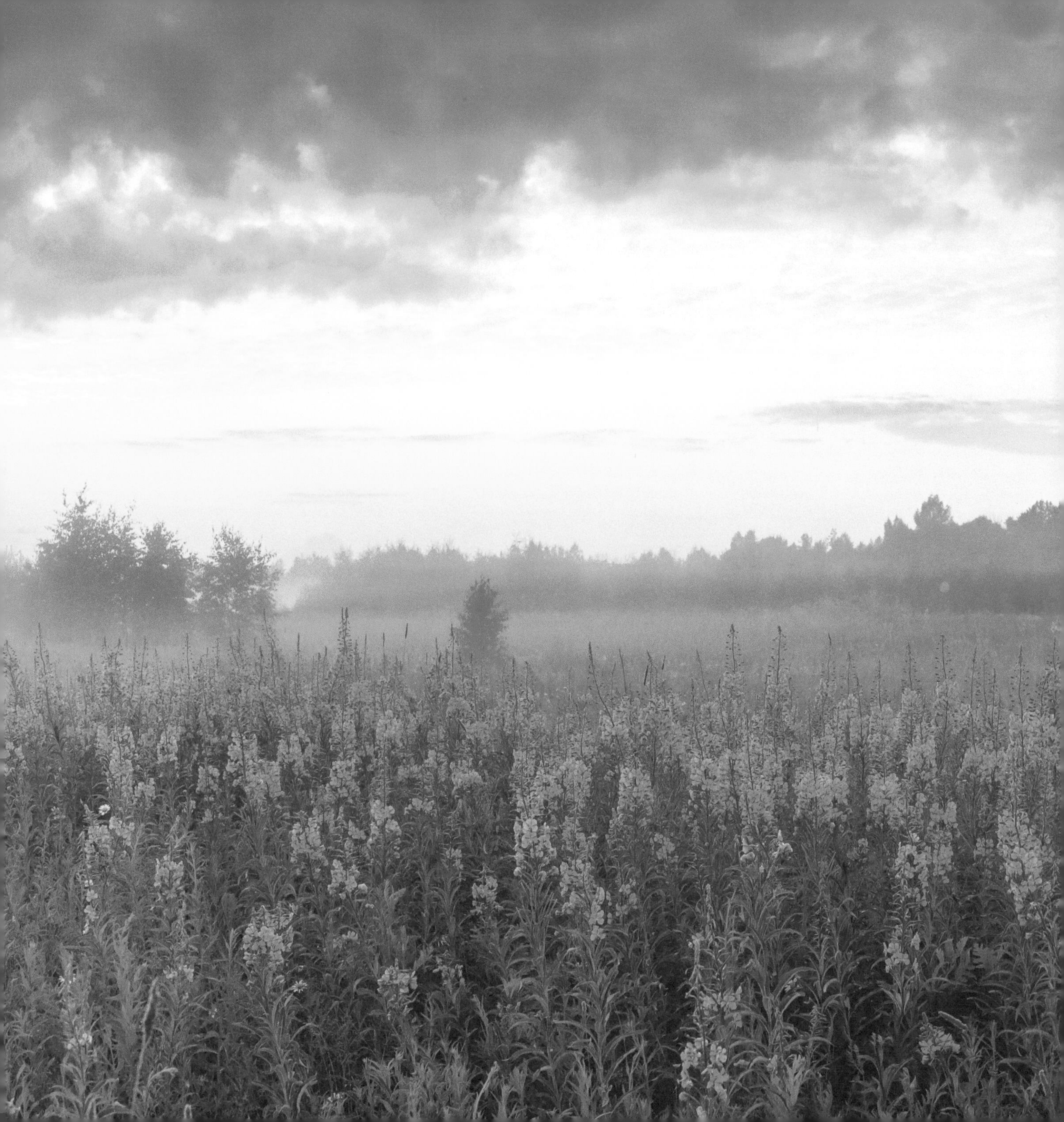

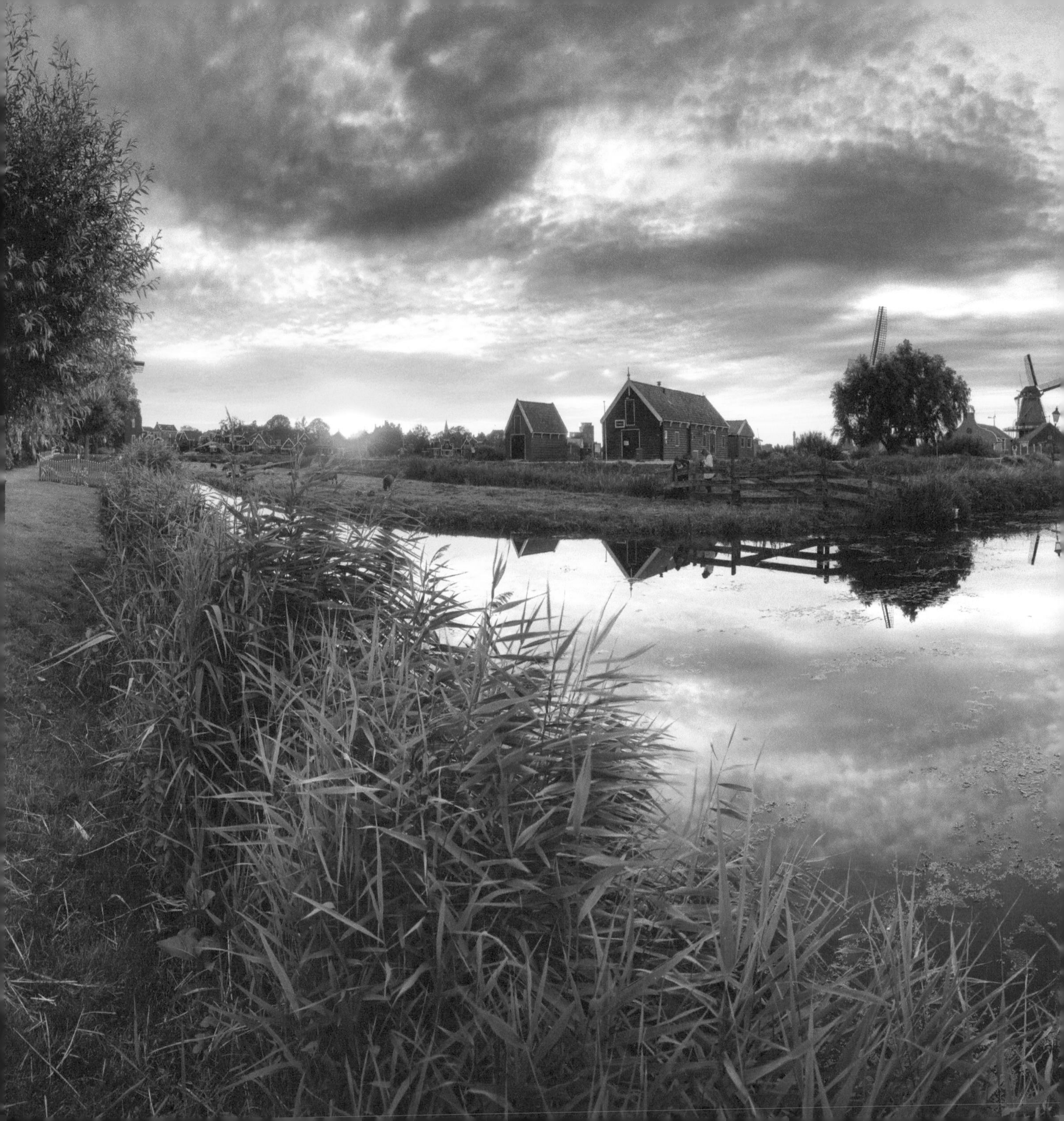

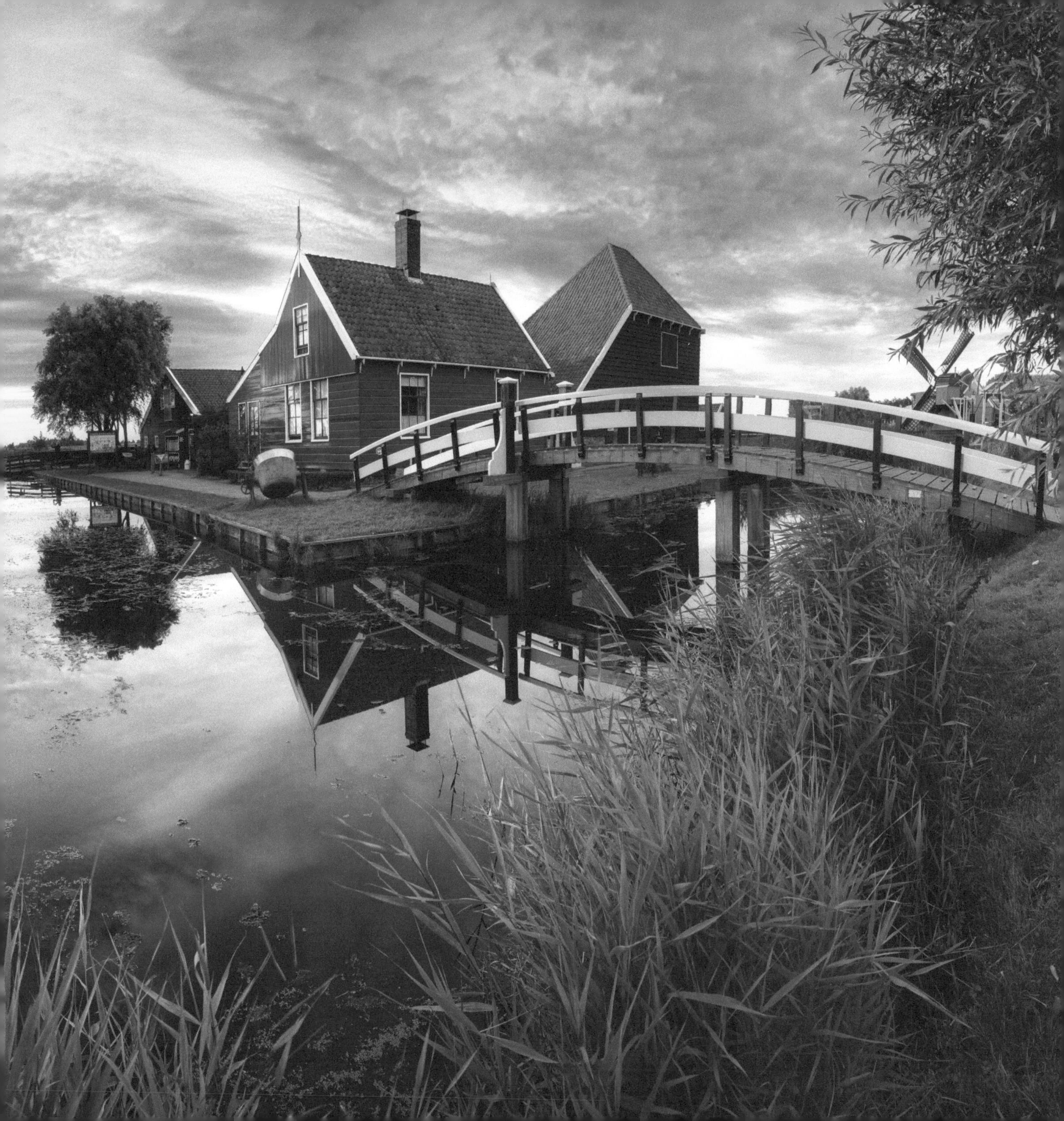

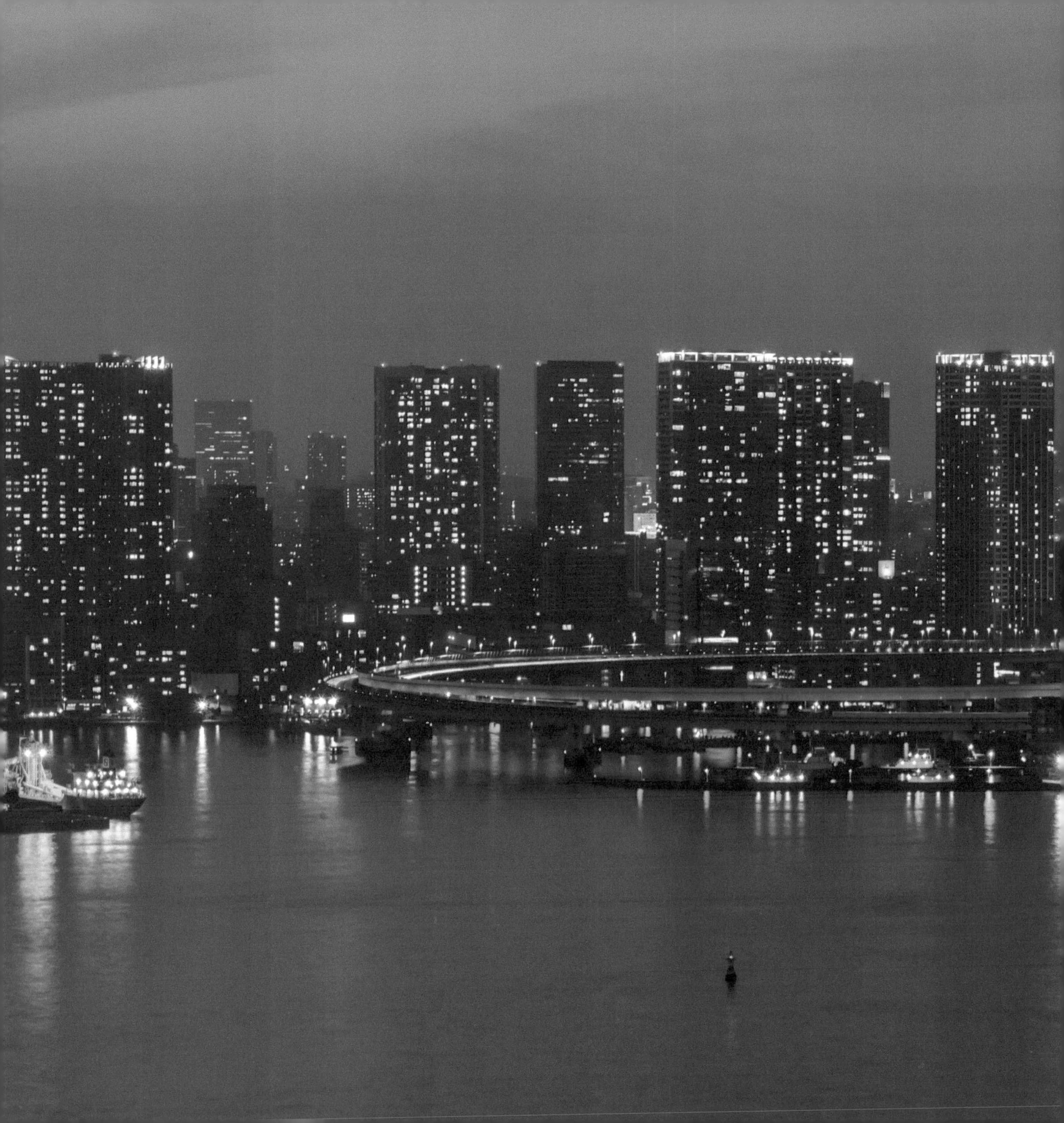

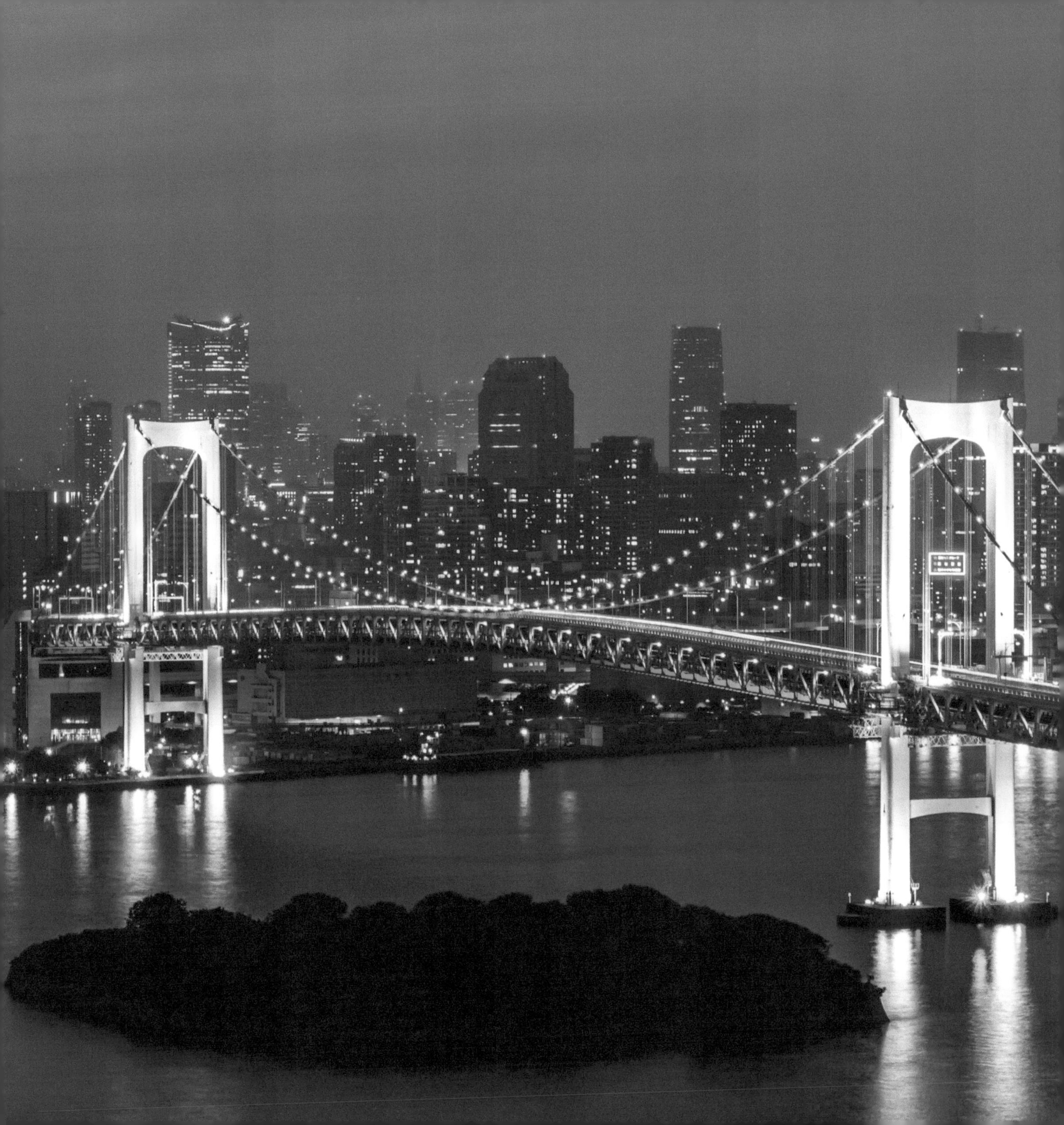

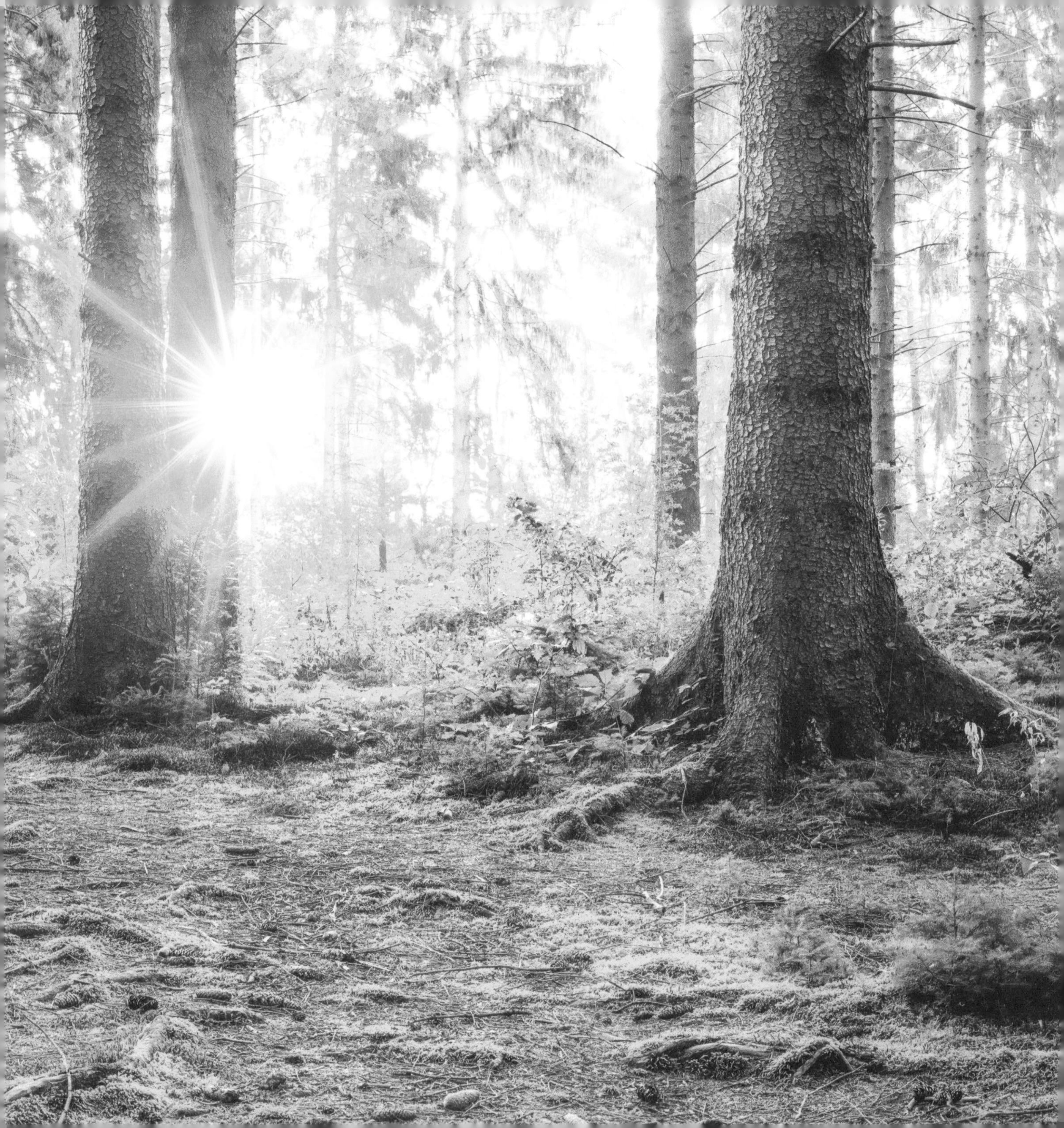

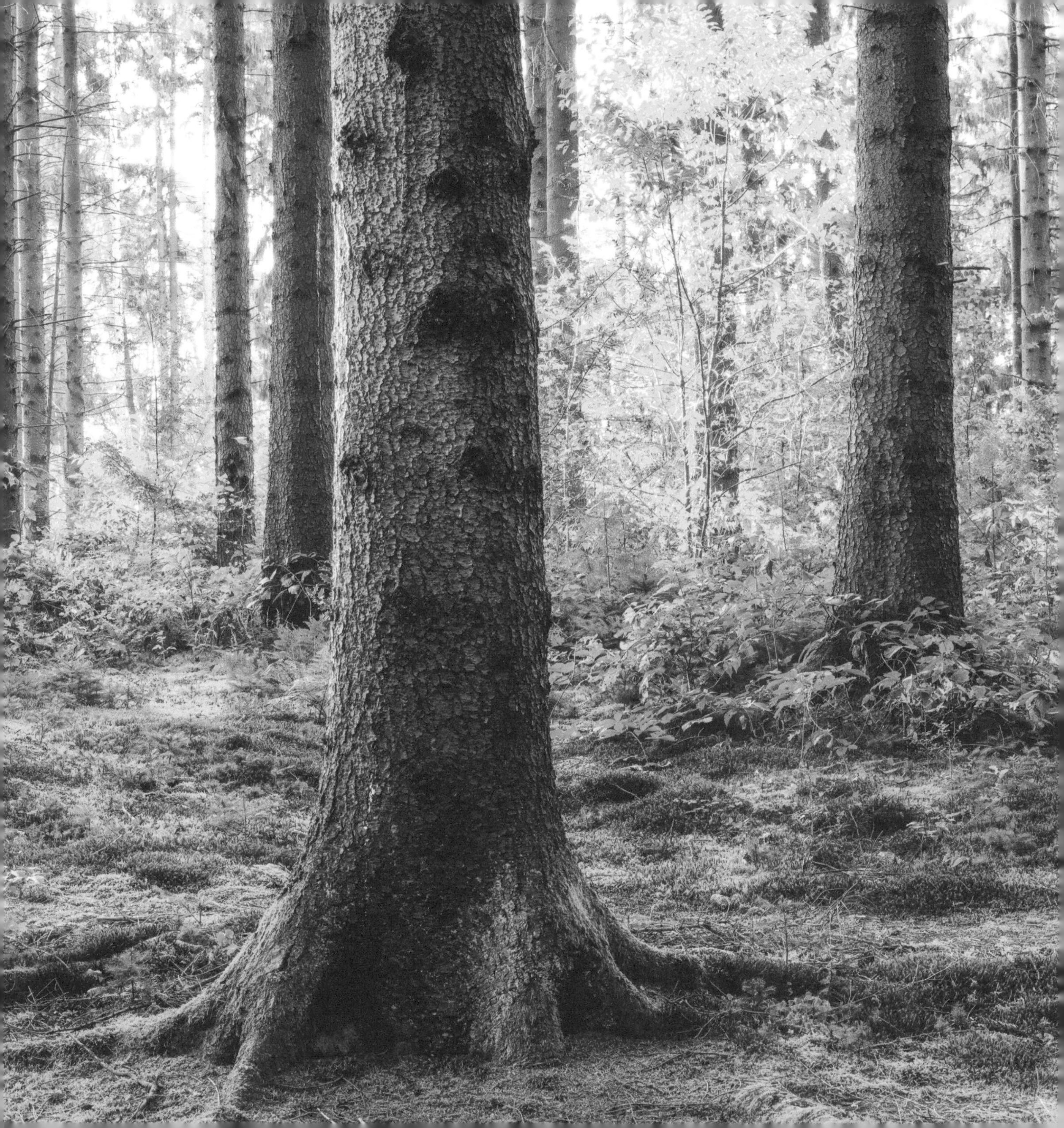

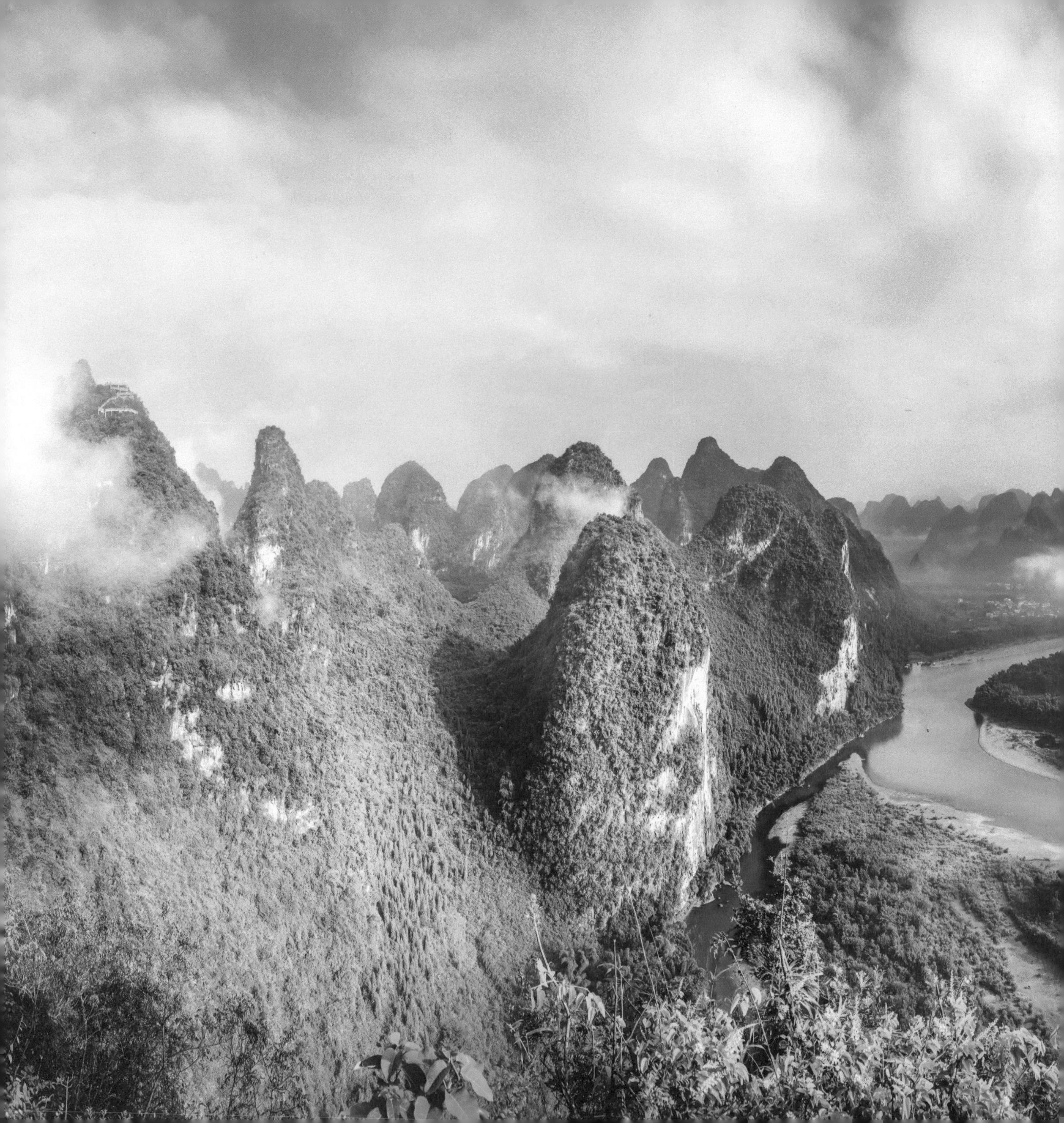

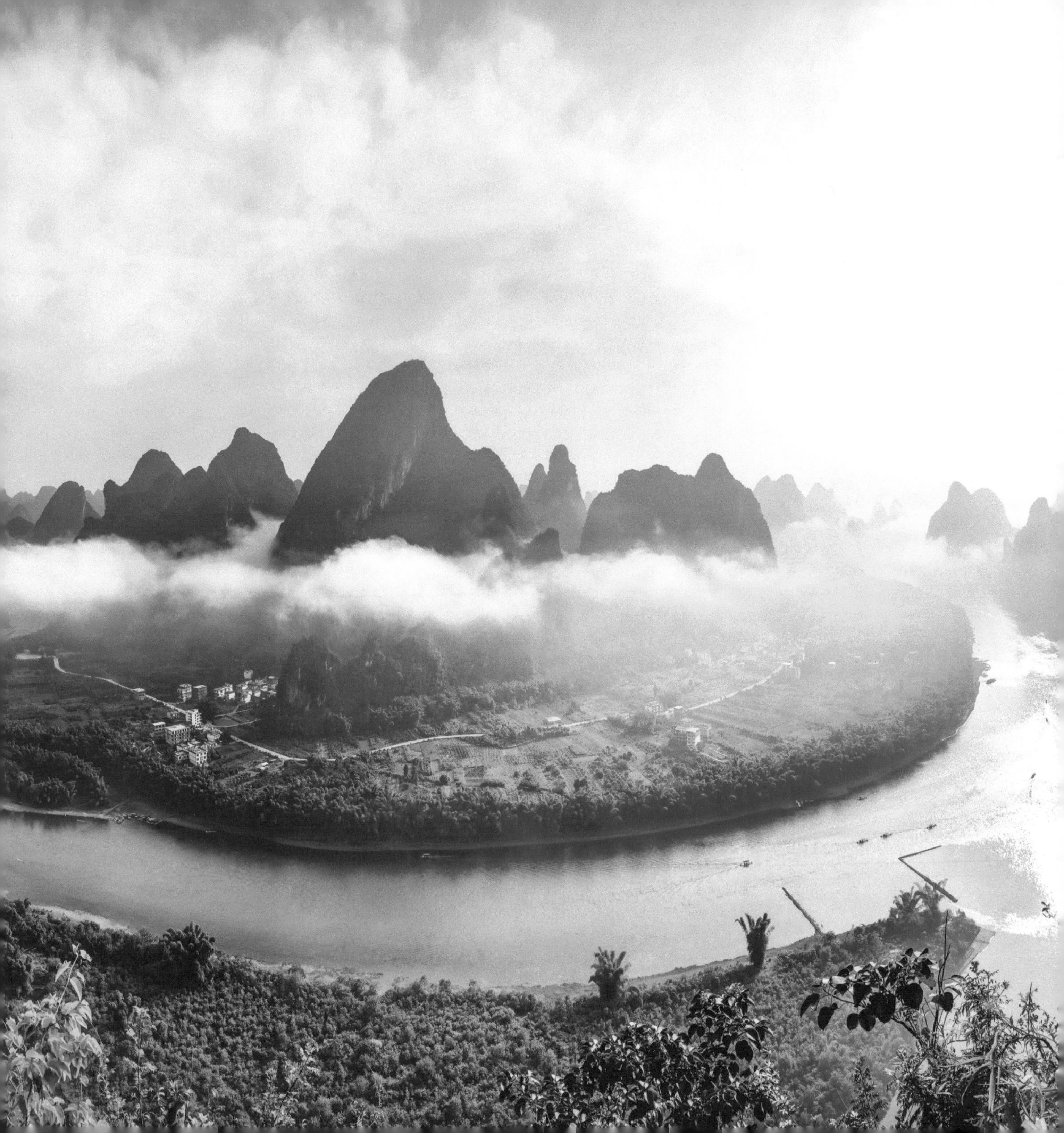

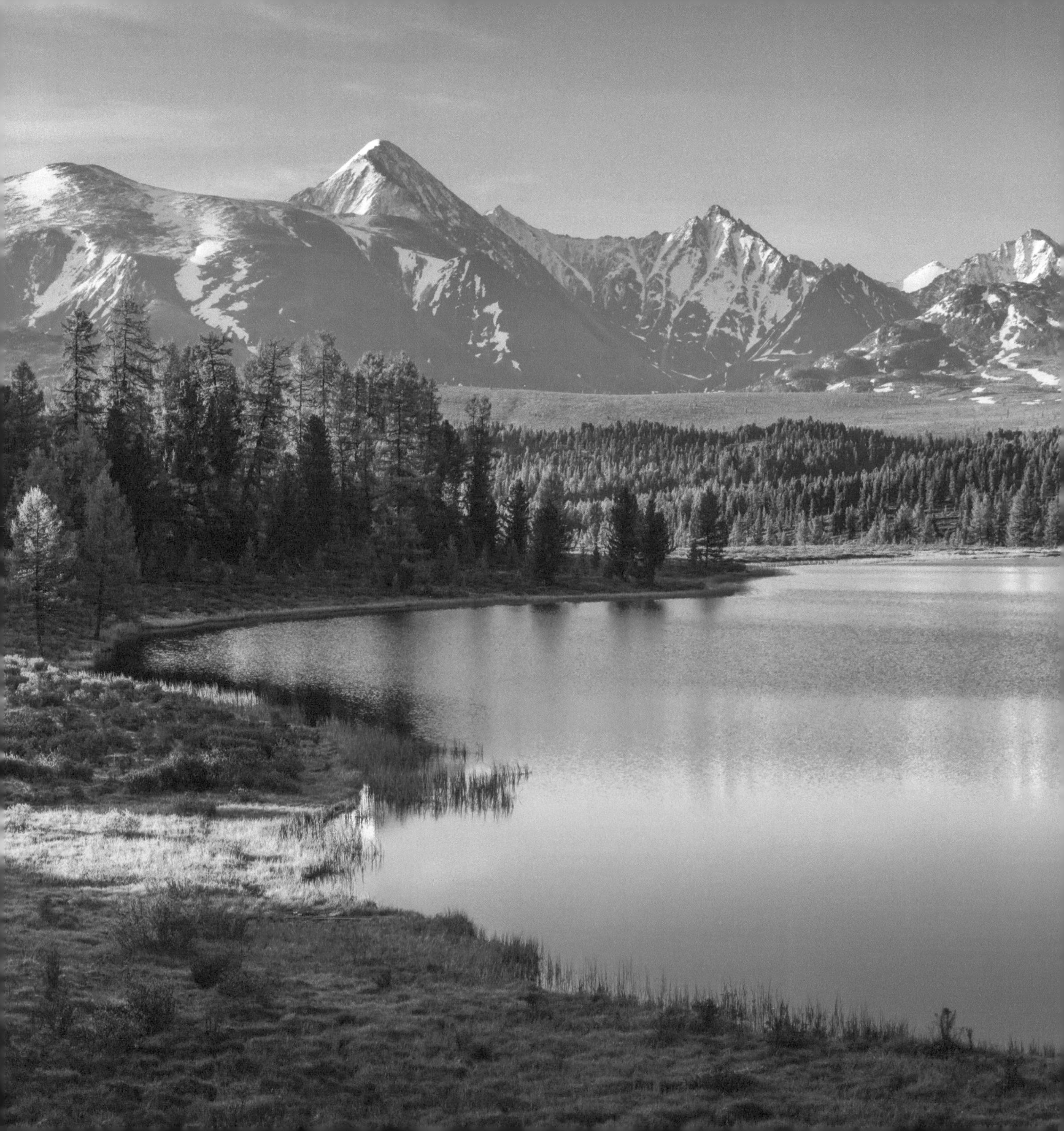

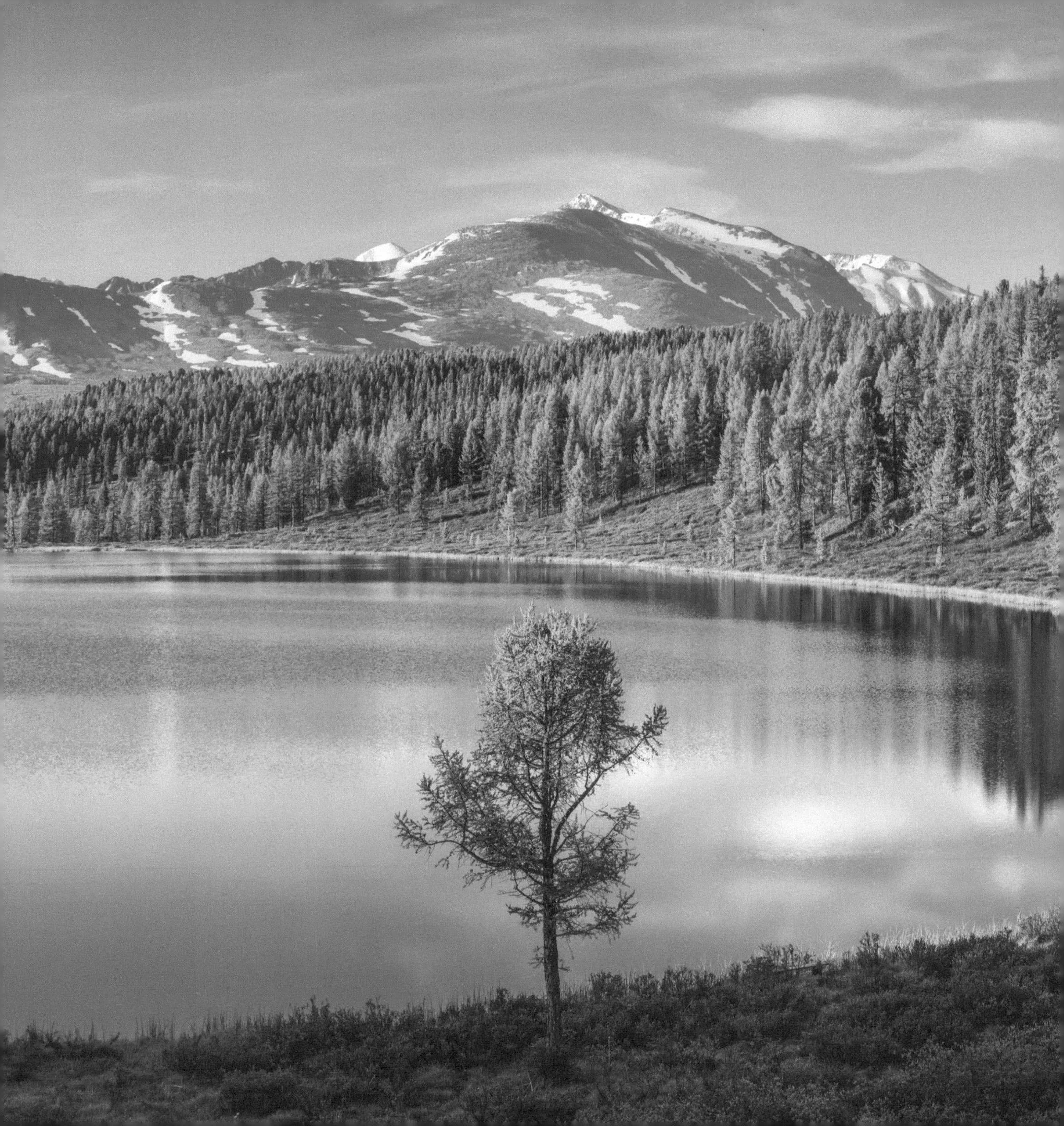

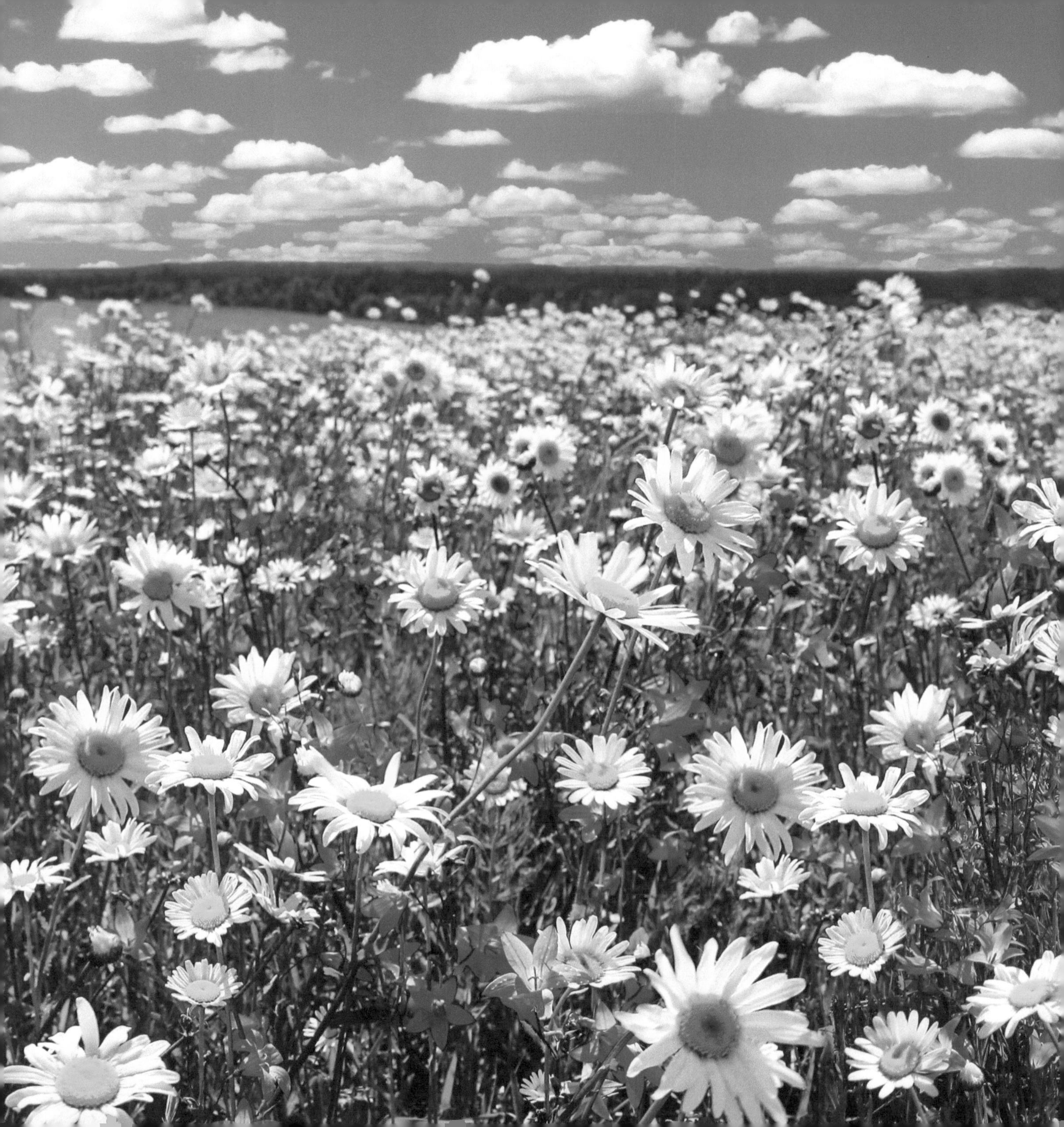

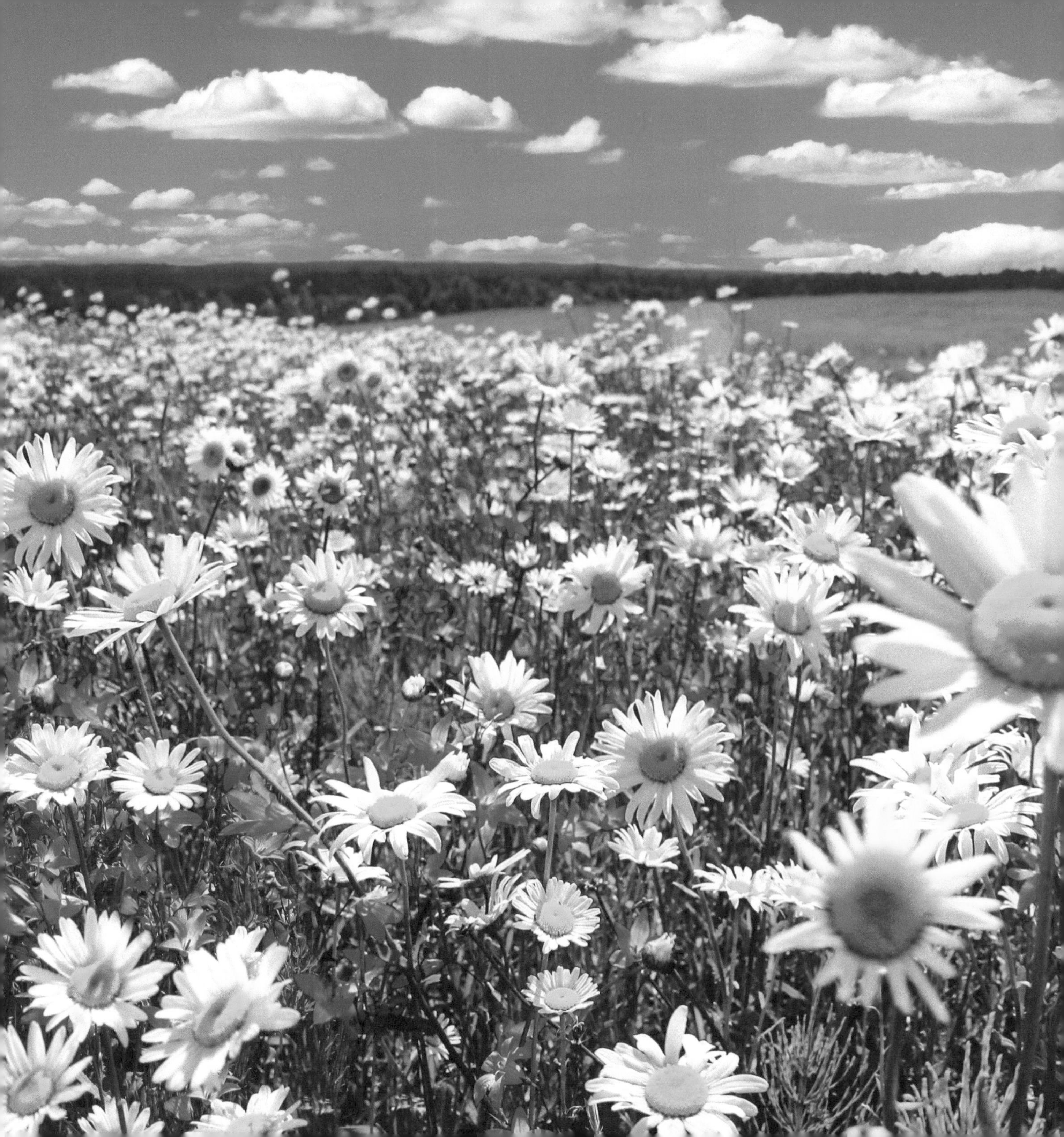

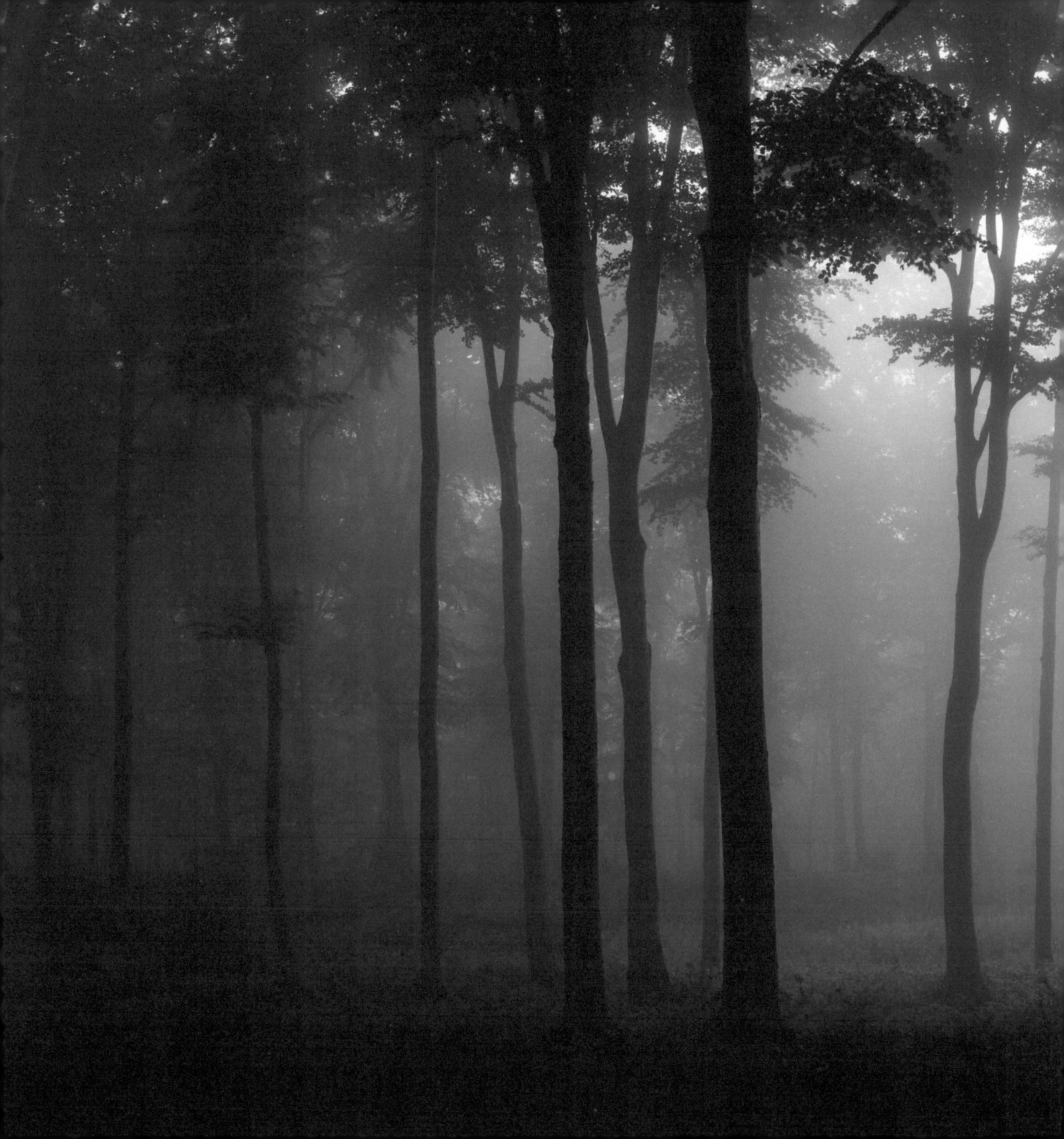

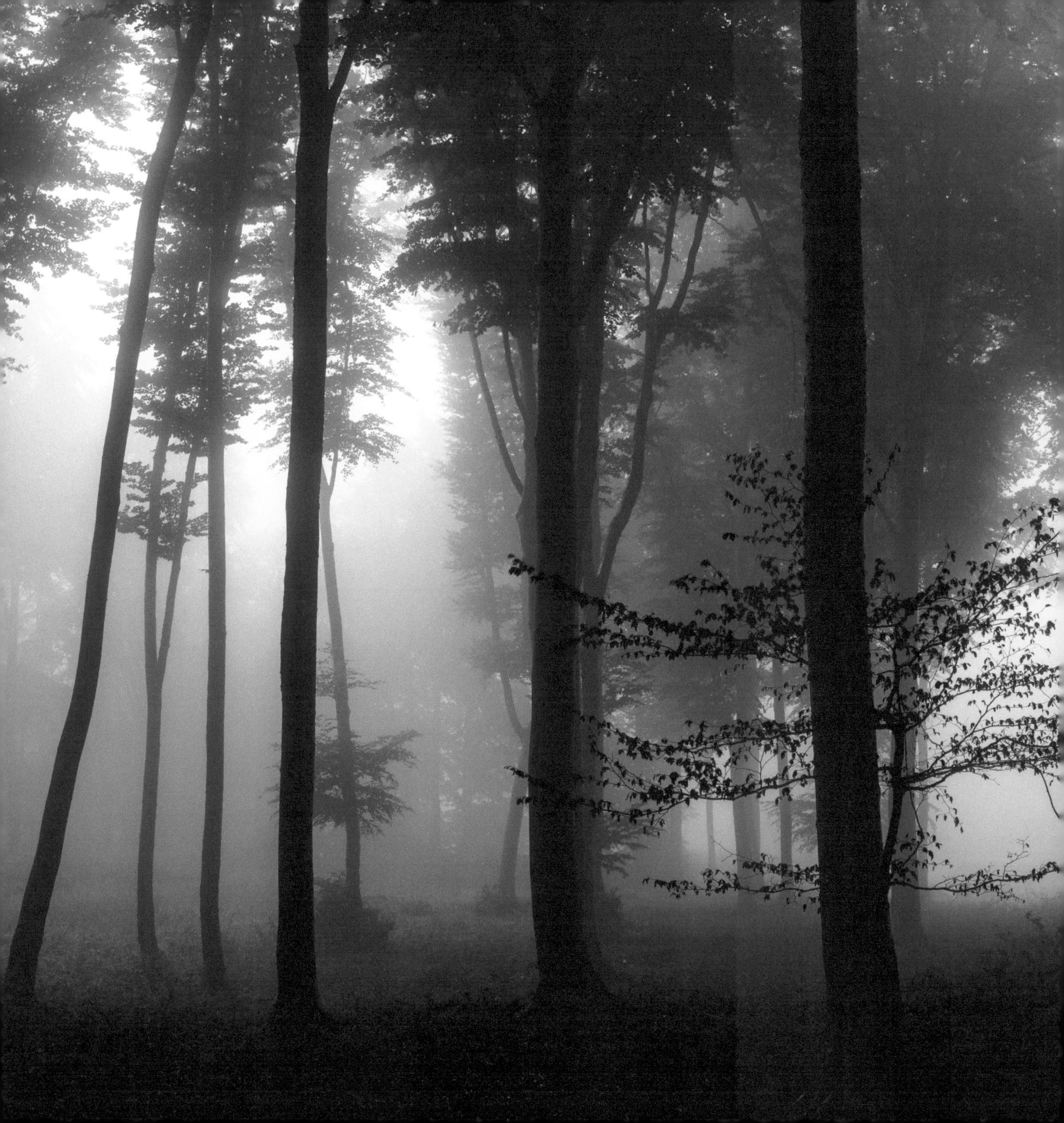

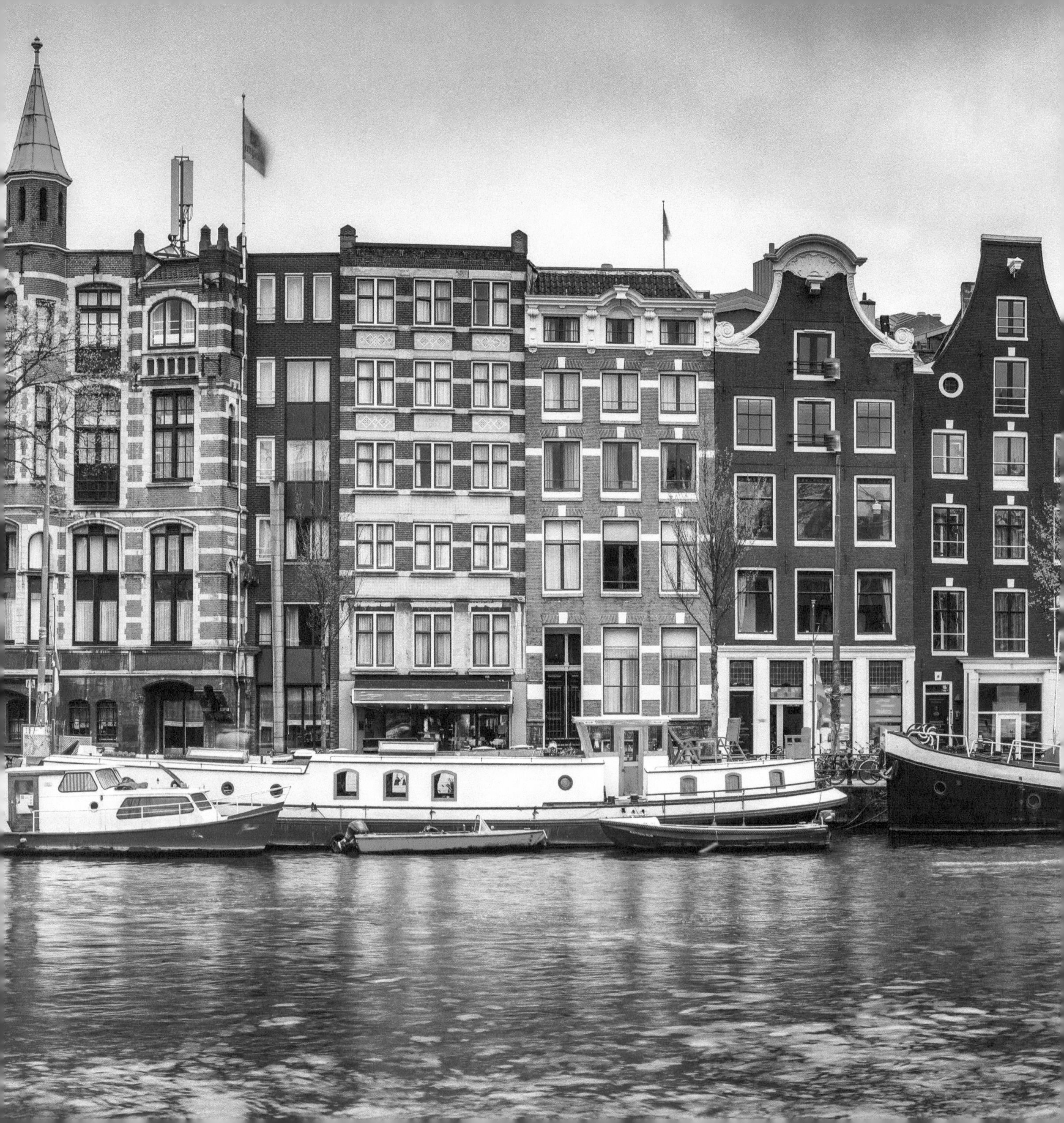

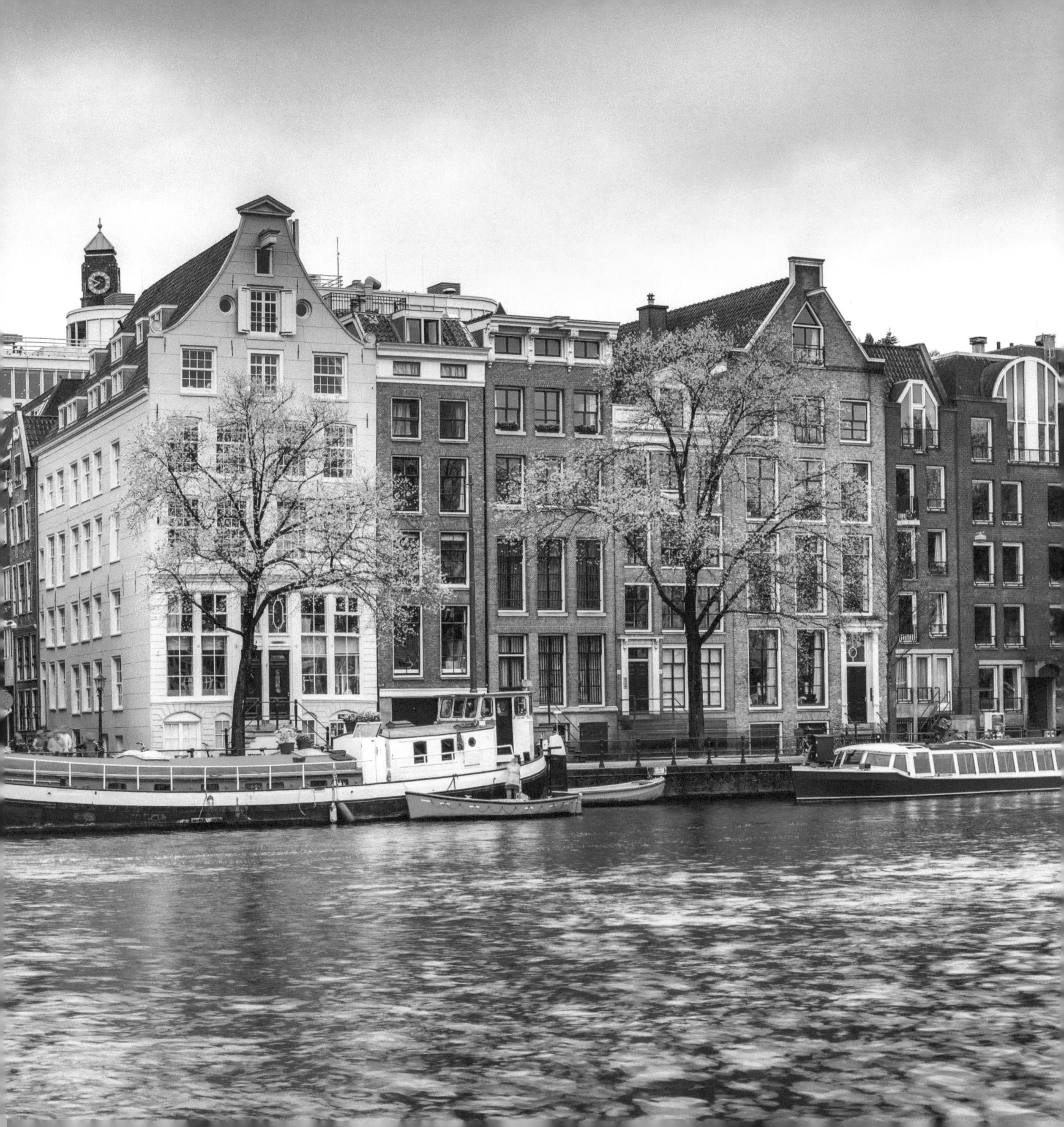

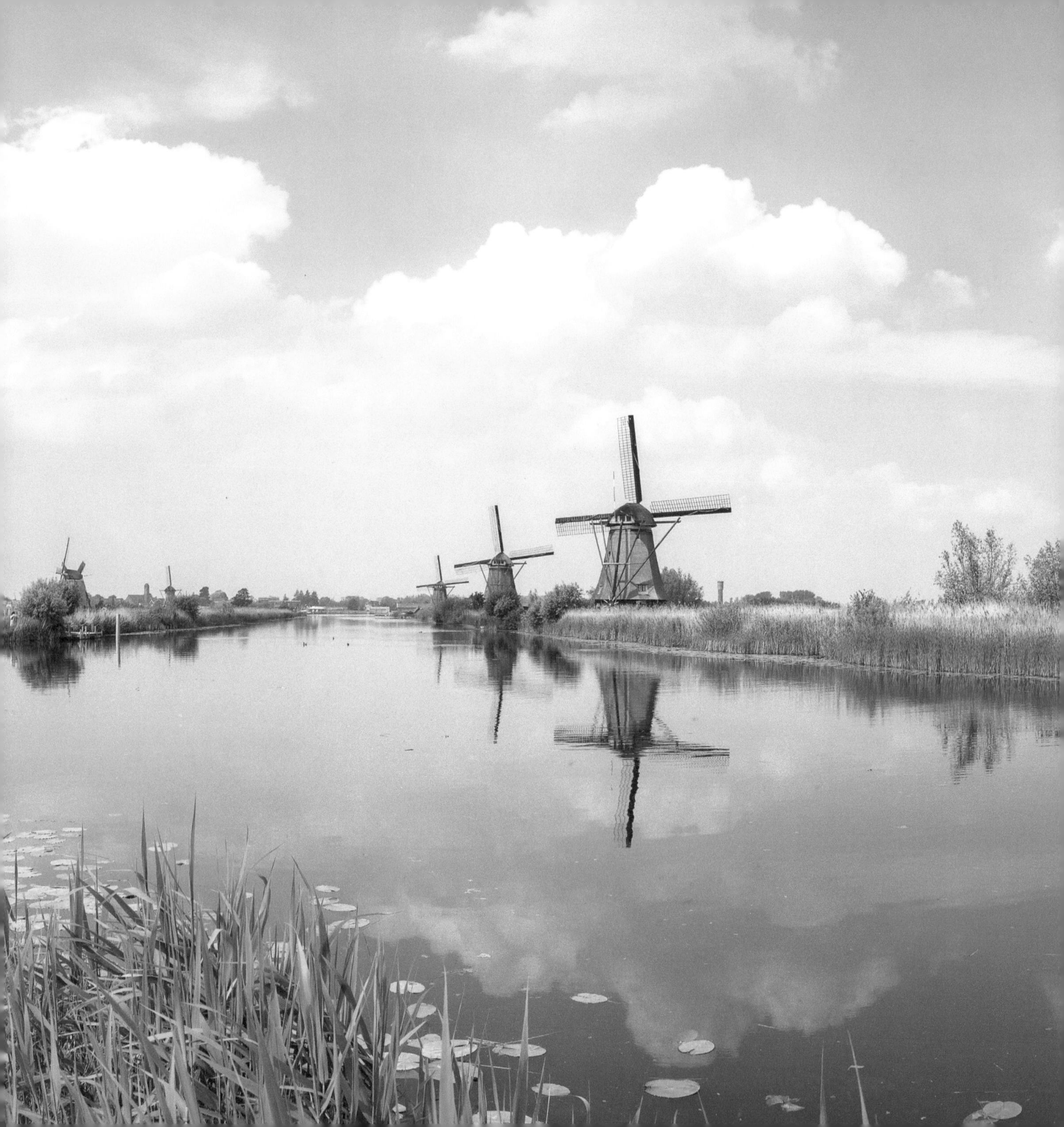

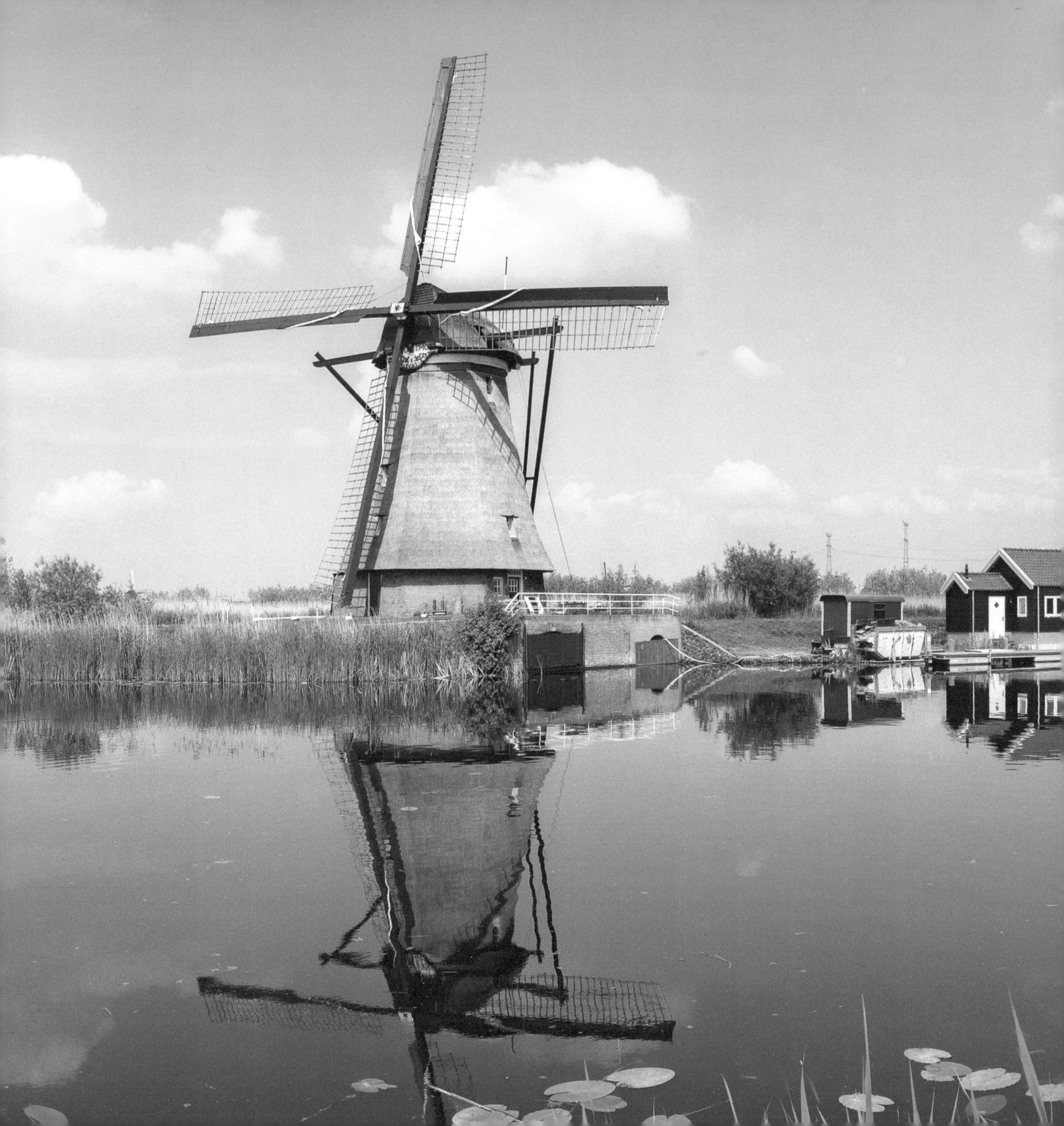

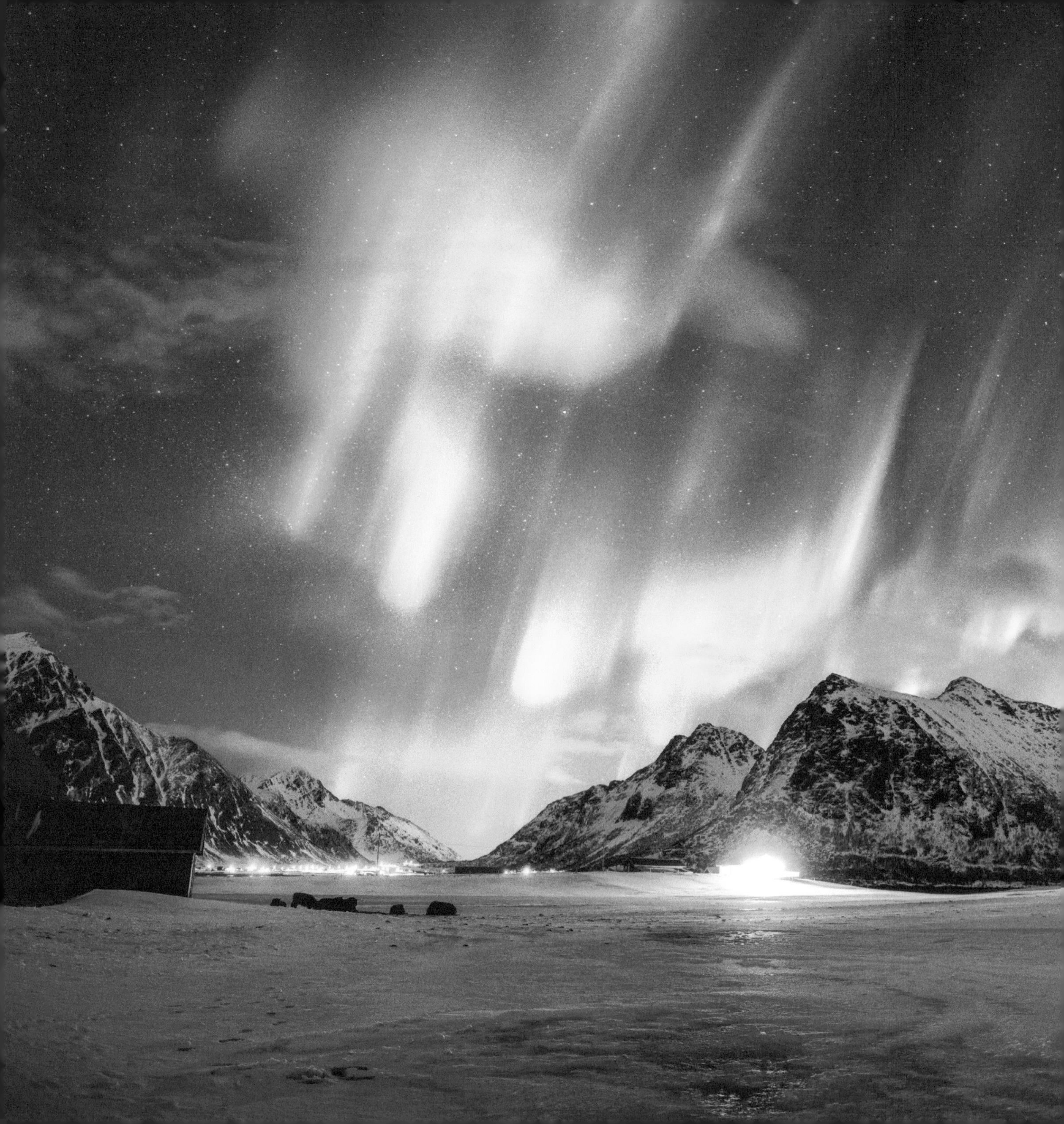